PLANNING A
WEDDING
RECEPTION
AT HOME

PLANNING A
WEDDING
RECEPTION
AT HOME

CAROL GODSMARK

howtobooks

Published by How To Books Ltd,
Spring Hill House, Spring Hill Road,
Begbroke, Oxford OX5 1RX, United Kingdom
Tel: (01865) 375794. Fax: (01865) 379162
info@howtobooks.co.uk
www.howtobooks.co.uk

How To Books greatly reduce the carbon footprint of their books by
sourcing their typesetting and printing in the UK.

British Library Cataloguing in Publication Data
A catalogue record for this book is available from the British Library

ISBN 978 1 84528 295 0

Cover design by Mousemat Design Limited
Cartoons by David Mostyn
Produced for How To Books by Deer Park Productions, Tavistock
Typeset by Pantek Arts Ltd, Maidstone, Kent
Printed and bound by Bell & Bain Ltd, Glasgow

NOTE: The material contained in this book is set out in good faith for
general guidance and no liability can be accepted for loss or expense
incurred as a result of relying in particular circumstances on statements
made in the book. Laws and regulations are complex and liable to change,
and readers should check the current position with the relevant authorities
before making personal arrangements.

Contents

Contents

To my darling daughter Caroline Godsmark and her partner
Barry Domedy who may be inspired by this book for their
forthcoming wedding, written with them and similarly placed
bridal couples in mind

Acknowledgements

My thanks and admiration go to Nikki Read of How to Books and to Melanie Jarman, my editor, for their wisdom, support and expertise.

I would also like to thank cartoonist David Mostyn whose apt, witty artwork raises a smile throughout the book.

Preface

The average UK wedding done by the book — venue, reception, musicians, vintage car, photographer, caterers, florists, toastmaster, stationary and, of course the wedding dress and rings — costs around £17,000. Then there's the honeymoon to pay for. But do weddings have to be as expensive as this?

One sure way of cutting down on skyrocketing costs is to cater for the wedding yourself and event-manage your venue. Brides, couples and families can take on this responsibility but often need a helping hand to make sure that the event — the most momentous day in the lives of the bride and groom — is a day to remember, and for all the right reasons!

Planning a Wedding Reception at Home takes you step-by-step through the whole process. As a professional caterer and event manager I will give you the low down on amounts of food and drink needed per guest, a timescale of when to buy and cook, how to present your creations to your guests, how to arrange for a marquee and staff as well as how to plan for the big day. You may wish to hire a caterer or do the catering yourself; both options are outlined in the book.

This book is for the inexperienced caterer who may have only cooked for friends and family, whether it be the bride, the bride and groom, or family or friends who wish to take on the catering in order to prepare a sit-down affair or a buffet for ten to 100. Throwing a memorable party without stress is definately achievable, and this book will show you how to control costs, create simple but terrific food, when to invite your guests, how many guests you can manage and even how to arrange a seating plan or the car parking.

All the little details that can be ironed out beforehand are also here, whether you are holding the reception at the home of the bride, her parents or friends, in a village hall or marquee.

Take the guesswork out of your special day! As an average, 40 percent of the wedding costs are spent on a hotel, restaurant or professionally catered-for marquee reception. This is an ideal book for controlling the wedding budget.

The principles in this book are also suitable for those catering for large parties such as birthday parties, christenings, bar mitzvahs, welcome home, graduation and other celebratory parties.

Within these page you will find:

- **Planning your wedding**: where to hold your reception of party; the advantages and challenges of holding either a summer or winter wedding; how many guests to invite; deciding on the catering; how formal or informal you wish your event to be; the wedding calendar of events and what is important — and not.

- **Budgeting**: paying for the wedding: preparing a realistic budget; getting quotations and estimates from key players (caterers, village hall hirers, marquee hire companies, florists, staff agencies); keeing records and keeping track of the costs. There will also be tips on how to have a less costly wedding.

- **Timing**: timing is all, your all-important checklist, time table, the order of the wedding day and restoring order after the day.

- **The all-important guest list**: paring the list down to suit space and budget; how to invite your guests (invitation possibilities and wording); dos and don'ts of the seating plan.

- **Your menu**: choosing your caterer or deciding to cater yourself; the types of meal to consider (from wedding breakfast to finger food reception); menu selection; the wedding cake.

- **Your chance to shine in the kitchen**: how to cook for ten or 200; how to choose that all-important menu; how to save on costs; how to source and order your food — and when; how to set out your food and organise food transport and safe storage; how to avoid food poisoning.

- **The all-important celebration drinks**: what will you offer your guests? Types of drinks to offer (and avoid); amounts to buy; how to manage the toasts; alcohol concerns.

- **Stage-managing the venue**: size of the marquee or hall; getting the space right for your occasion; ordering equipment; tips for dealing with suppliers; making the venue come alive with deco-rations; orgainising staff and transport.

- **Getting the most out of your staff**: how to choose and manage staff; dress and behaviour code; being kind to your staff.

- **The party's over**: tying up loose ends; thank you letters; invoice-paying; post wedding party.

My aim in writing this book is to ensure that you have as smooth a ride as possible in transforming your home, marquee, village hall or other venue into a welcoming place for your guests.

My aim is also to ensure that you and your family and friends directly involved in your wedding or celebration, are well-versed in how to run the event. Stress-levels can be banished to a huge extent from your lives; everyone can enjoy the day when it arrives and you can give yourself a big pat on the back for creating this memorable time together.

As a caterer and event manager for a variety of different events such as film festivals, fundraising parties, funerals, gallery talks, food conferences, 100th birthday party weekend celebrations, film shoot catering, orchestra corporate parties and many other events, including numerous weddings, I wish to share my experiences of running such events with you. My knowledge of food comes from these sources as well as my experience of cooking in my own resturant and catering company for the past twenty years.

I hope you will find all that you need within these pages. A final tip: keeping a sense of humour and perspective is as essential as the time you set aside to plan your big day.

1 Planning your wedding

Congratulations! You've decided on the big day and would like to celebrate. But the budget, due to commitments such as the mortgage, may be less than sparkling. What are the choices regarding the all-important party? You can, of course, go to a hotel or restaurant and pay for the privilege, or hire a caterer and a venue such as a village hall. Or you could put up a marquee in a garden or book the village hall and do the catering yourself. Doing your own catering would certainly keep down the costs. But who in their right mind would choose to cater for their own wedding?

It might seem like a crazy idea, but why not? There are few people who wish to spend a small fortune on just the one day to mark the rest of their lives together. The average cost of a wedding in Britain is around the £17,000 mark with some 40 per cent of the costs going to the caterer, be it in a hotel, restaurant or for a professionally catered for marquee reception. London's costs will be approximately 15% higher.

You may find it too daunting a prospect being involved with the food and may wish to book a caterer but do the other arrangements, such as hiring the venue, getting quotes for a marquee, arranging the transport, sending out the invitations, hiring staff, finding the perfect cake-maker and ordering the champagne, yourself.

Since I'm sure you don't want to start your new life together on the wrong foot – in debt from day one – it would be a wise move to eliminate part of the expense. Examine both possibilities – to cater or not to cater yourself – and get organised.

This chapter will cover:

- a look at the types of locations
- a checklist of questions to ask the hirer of the location
- summer versus winter for your wedding
- a look at your guest list
- catering for your wedding

- going formal or staying informal

- your wedding plan calendar of events

- the order of the wedding day

- timing is all: the bride and groom's time list and the venue timing

- compiling your all-important contacts list

- car hire

- keeping a level head — what's important and what's not worth the fuss.

Deciding on the location for the reception

Your first decision is where you both wish to hold your reception. Possible locations range from your home, perhaps either parents' homes if you're in that age bracket, or a generous friend or relative who will lend you their home, or a marquee put up in the garden in one of these venues. Another option is your local village hall. But there are plenty of other types of venues to consider, some of which are more unusual and memorable. Use the internet to search for 'wedding venues for hire', check out your *Yellow Pages* and local library, canvass friends or try weddingvenues.com for further inspiration.

Here are some suggestions:

- **Barn for hire**: a delightful, casual, sometimes spacious venue, with many in a pretty setting.

- **Village halls**: Look outside your immediate area for inspiration if you aren't keen on your local village hall.

- **Golf club**: some provide the catering, others hire out the premises only.

- **Railway stations**: yes, it is sometimes possible to hold parties on the platform or in the booking hall, for example.

- **Leisure centres**: delve into your *Yellow Pages* to start the search.

- **Castles and forts**: some may offer the space but not the catering.

- **Mines**: a most remarkable venue; Poldark Mine in Cornwall is just one wedding setting to be had around the country.

When you start looking you may also find details of pumping stations, gardens, pavilions and other places. Some of them offer catering, others just the space with or without equipment such as chairs and tables and other necessities.

Researching your location

You need to take into consideration the venue where your wedding reception will take place. You have a finite space for your guests, unless you are outdoors, hence the need to know how many you will be catering for.

Points to look out for when choosing a venue:

- How much parking space is there and is the entrance convenient for the caterer to unload the food and drink?

- What is the access to the venue within the building like? Are there a lot of stairs to negotiate for carrying up food, drink, equipment, chairs, tables, cutlery, glasses, flowers and other items?

- How many chairs and tables are there? Are there enough?

- How clean is the venue?

- Is there an alcohol licence? Until what time? If not, can we supply the champagne and wine but pay a corkage charge?

- How easy is it to access the building on the day? Do you need to go through a caretaker or will you be given keys?

- How many hours can you hire it for? Is there another party booked either before or after you?

- What is included in the deal? Is VAT included, for example?

- How do you lock up if the caretaker doesn't do this for you?

- What health and safety measures are in place? (exits, fire extinguishers)

- What deposit is required and what is the cancellation charge?

Tip

In some village halls you are expected to pay for lighting with some of the older ones having meters. Find out about lighting and heating when talking to the manager.

You will also have to know what kind of kitchen you will be able to finish preparing your food in (the vast majority of the cooking will have taken place in the caterer's kitchen or your own).

Points to look out for include:

- How clean and well looked after is the kitchen?

- Are there sufficient sinks, a freezer, a fridge?

- Will the cooker meet your needs? Does it have enough burners and ovens? Is it easy to light or do you need a demonstration?

- Does the kitchen have enough prepping space or are there few working surfaces?

- Does the venue offer equipment and, if so, what are the plates, cutlery and glasses like? Are there enough for your guests? Count everything just to make sure.

- Are there enough — if any — serving dishes or will you need to bring your own?

- Does the venue supply washing up liquid and any other cleaning materials including dishcloths and tea towels?

- Is there a sufficient amount of hot water or is the boiler not up to scratch?

- Are there health and safety measures in place such as exits, fire blankets, fire extinguishers?

- Make sure when viewing the kitchen where the food will be finished off and served that you note how many rings and ovens there are as you don't want to be juggling pots and pans trying to heat up food in time.

- Make sure too when viewing the kitchen that you have enough refrigeration and that the fridge is plugged in well before your party so that it is at the right temperature (4°C). Some village halls and other venues, in order to save on electricity, unplug everything.

Other questions which may be useful also include:

- Do you book in other parties — will there be a time constraint on our event?

- What is the setting like for photography? (Are you seeking a lakeside setting, for example?)

- What facilities are there if the weather is poor?

- Is there outside space for a summer wedding? Heating for a winter wedding?

- What is the parking like?

- How many toilets are there? You do not wish to have guests queuing because of insufficient toilet facilities.

- Is there a coat area and space for presents?

- Is there disabled access? You may have guests in wheelchairs, for example.

- Do you have a PA system for speeches or for musicians?

- Can we book our own musicians and florists?

- Do you have a seating plan stand?

- Can we throw confetti?

- Do you allow professional firework displays at your venue?

- Are you licenced for holding marriage ceremonies? You may wish to get married where the reception will be instead of in a church or registry office.

- Do you have special arrangements with local taxi companies?

- Can I have references from clients who have used the venue?

Other practicalities to consider before viewing the venues

Narrow down several venues in your area and visit them.

But before you do, make sure the dates you have in mind are available at the venue. Otherwise, you may have a wasted journey. If you are flexible, ask for alternative dates too.

- Is the location suitable for your guests?

- How far away is it from the church or registry office?

- Look for cleanliness. (Is the kitchen clean? Is the entrance inviting or marked and dirty?)

- Is the space suitable for your wedding if you plan to have a stage, music, dancing or other entertainment?

- Logistically, how will it work for you if you are doing the catering? Is there good storage space for drinks, an area for the bar, easy access to the kitchen area from the car or van, and adequate washing up facilities?

- Is it convenient to pick up the keys and return them if it is a village hall, for example? You don't want to be trudging all over the countryside trying to locate the keyholder.

- If you're interested in the venue, take clear details of who to contact if you wish to make a firm booking. Get an agreement in writing if you proceed, with all the points covered (such as cost, VAT, length of hire, equipment included in the cost, parking spaces, key return if applicable).

Tip

You may have to be flexible if you want to hire the place you feel happiest with. Book well in advance if possible. Be flexible too in regard to what both of you want — and what the budget will stand.

Get married on a week day as many venues are cheaper than on weekends.

Getting married later on in the day cuts down on your costs as you will only have one meal to cater for. Some wedding parties sit down to lunch followed by supper in the evenings pre or post dancing.

Deciding when to get married

Planning a winter wedding

Increasingly, winter weddings are becoming more popular for both practical and pleasurable reasons. Out of season venues are cheaper to hire,
you have a better pick if deciding to marry at shorter notice and costs
are generally lower all-round as caterers, keen on getting winter bookings, will offer you a better deal with hopefully the same quality-led
food. You can also find wintery scenery (Scotland abounds with glori-
ously frosty or snowy vistas) and fireplaces with blazing logs add to the
romance. Homely, comfort food (cheaper to buy and easier to serve:
think of coq au vin, boeuf Bourguignonne or a glamorous fish pie with
puff pastry and herb cream sauce) can also make a winter wedding one
to consider.

> **Tip**
>
> Winter wedding in marquees are becoming more and more popular;
> marquees are now easily adapted to cope with the wet and the cold.

You may also get away with having a quieter wedding with fewer guests in
winter if it is what you would prefer. A summer wedding can be seen as
more hedonistic and big, with many friends and family – and work colleagues – all joining in. If your conscience gets to you, invite those not on
the wedding list to a drinks reception later on. It is, after all, *your* wedding,
not your parents', parents'-in-law or your best friend's – all of whom may
wish to influence you. As there are fewer weddings in winter, yours will
stand out and be a real treat during those dark days for all your guests. Do
avoid the clichéd Valentine's Day wedding, however. Catering and other
costs go up for this cheesy calendar date. Strive for originality.

I would also try to avoid just after Christmas. This period is fraught with problems, not least seasonal greetings fatigue, caterer fatigue, guest list turmoil ('Sorry, but we always go skiing', 'We always stay with auntie Bertha in the Gower Peninsula', 'Can we bring Flo, Marcus and Desdemona, our house guests?'). Your Christmas will be taken over by lists, plans and sleepless nights.

Deciding on a summer wedding

Summer weddings are the option taken by many people due to hoped-for clement weather, longer nights and the possibility of holding the reception out of doors, although this can never be guaranteed. But summer weddings can be more costly for the reasons given above. If your budget is tight, it may be a good idea to review having a summer one, or to have a smaller celebration. But, should you have your heart set on a summer wedding, there are ways to minimise expenses.

Your guest list

The guest list will be covered in more depth in Chapter 3, but as part of this overview, we need to take the numbers of guests into the equation. As you are looking at venues and considering general costs at this preliminary stage, you'll need to consider your guest list first in order to decide on the size of the venue.

In the initial excitement of becoming engaged and setting a date, it is customary to want to spread your happiness to all and sundry, and share the day with a large group of friends, family and work colleagues. Hold back right now! Now is the time to be ruthless. Your spend per head will escalate out of control if you put down everyone in your address book. Be selective. You can always have a smaller wedding with a larger party after your marriage thereby ignoring no one you would like to include in your festivities.

Catering for your wedding

Your budget will have a major impact on the type of catering you can enjoy. Your first decision is whether to have a professional caterer or tackle the catering yourself. This doesn't mean you will do it alone — family and friends' culinary abilities will be given the chance to shine. Now is the time to work out what spend per head you envisage. At this stage it will be a rough estimate, be it from a professional caterer's quotes or your own figures.

Tip

Your guests will appreciate a quality meal of simplicity rather than a complicated affair with expensively decorated tables.

You may like to offer your guests lunch, be it a three course meal or buffet. Or you may opt for a finger food reception, a three course dinner with all the trimmings. Will you be offering food too if music and dancing are part of the late-night equation? Put an approximate sum against each person on your guest list for the food alone and add it up. This doesn't include drink and is an excellent way of starting to cull the guest list.

Chapter 2 (budgeting) and Chapter 6 (menu choice) will help you make a decision about the catering.

Formal or informal?

Formal weddings

Formal weddings are more costly of course. From quality dresses, shoes, tiaras, men's formal attire, limos, flowers, printed invitations, a toast-master, musicians, champagne and upmarket catering, to say nothing of the choice of venue. Formal weddings can also be highly stressful if not managed with foresight and clarity. By having a small, formal wedding, many of the above costs are minimised, and you can still have a delightful, memorable wedding.

Informal weddings

If you choose to organise a more informal wedding without observing the conventions that go with more formal affairs, there are ways of saving money. For example:

- Choose clothing that you will continue to wear at smart occasions.

- Buy your own flowers from a wholesaler and arrange them yourself or with the help of family members.

- Ask a gifted friend to bake a cake as a wedding present.

- Decorate the village hall or marquee with flowers taken from the church or registry office once the marriage service is over.

- Have more informal music, played by live musicians.

The catering, either done professionally or by you, can be simpler and more relaxed. You could, for example, offer guests a two-course buffet or finger food, and provide well-chosen wines you've brought over from France or have bought from your local wine shop (which is prepared to negotiate a good deal). Instead of a seating plan you may prefer to provide a general guide to seating. An informal wedding does of course need to be just as meticulously planned as a formal wedding so that guests know where to go and when, and that staff or family are primed to ensure that everything goes to plan.

Creating a wedding plan calendar

To ensure that you are able to plan your wedding day with the least possible stress it is very important to create a wedding plan calendar and keep to the schedules.

Once you have decided on the date, start canvassing your friends, colleagues and family for their caterers', musicians', florists' and photographers' recommendations.

Start combing websites, *Yellow Pages* and other sources to widen your search for the most appropriate companies to deal with. When phoning them, have the check list on pages 4–7 handy and a further list of questions you wish to ask also written down. Then you can systematically check them off so that you have an instant database of information rather than little scraps of paper with confusing details. Buy a notebook where you can store your information and keep it handy.

The lists below are general ones, and probably not all points will be applicable to you. Also, I have not added points such as choosing the best man or bridesmaids, for example, as this book caters primarily for the catering and event management of your wedding or celebration.

Nine to six months prior to the wedding

- Create your first guest list, but be prepared to cull it.

- Get quotes and book the wedding venue and where the wedding ceremony is to be held. Carefully read over the agreement and ensure that all costs are present and correct. Make sure the VAT is added on so you won't get a nasty surprise with the final invoice.

- Get quotes from caterers and book the company. Ensure a contract is drawn up with all the details of the menu, equipment, staff, costs (to include VAT), time, venue details, contact details.

Also make sure you know when down payments and the final payment are due.

- Get quotes from marquees and agree on arrangements.
- Get quotes from photographers and check their availability.
- Get quotes from musicians and check their availability.
- Start looking for the accommodation for the wedding party.
- Decide on the flowers: visit florists and get prices.
- Start considering where the honeymoon will be.

Six to three months prior to the wedding

- Finalise the guest list and send out invitations at least two or three months prior to the wedding.
- Decide on the style of the invitations and get quotes for the printing and any other printing work you may need such as place name cards.
- Book the accommodation for the wedding party.
- Finalise musicians' and photographers' bookings.
- Get quotes for the cake and book it in writing with all details and delivery.
- If doing the catering yourself, start working on the menu and making a list of supplies and suppliers.
- Get quotes for any transportation requirements and book the cars in writing with full details (time, where, when, who is to go in each car, cost including VAT).
- Book the florists and finalise details of types of flowers, delivery and time.
- Book the honeymoon.

A month prior to the wedding

- Check over details of the caterers, the venue and other major arrangements and adjust any details if necessary.

- Check to see if you have arrangements with all the companies you are dealing with in writing. If not, ask them for a detailed letter or contract and go through it, making sure that the timing, date and every last point has been addressed.

- Make up a timetable and schedule for the big day.

- Compile a contact list for the day from caterers to cars (see a sample list on page 19).

- Keep tabs on the guest list and contact those who haven't replied.

- Inform the caterers and reception venue of final numbers a week in advance (or whatever they have stipulated in the agreement).

- Finalise the seating plan if you are having one.

- Decide who will be doing which tasks to make the days prior to the wedding and the day itself go smoothly.

- Sort out who is sitting where in the church or registry office and make a plan. Discuss this with those involved. You may wish to reserve the two front rows on either side of the aisle in the church, for example, for both sets of family placed on opposite sides. Ushers should be informed of the list.

The order of the wedding day

This list can help you to focus on your day. The timing is broken down to suit the bride, groom, ceremony venue and reception venue.

12.00 p.m: marriage ceremony in Chichester registry office

1.00 p.m: photographs in the park

2.00 p.m: wedding breakfast

4.00 p.m: toasts and speeches

5.00 p.m: music from the band

7.30 p.m: evening reception commences

8.00 p.m: evening disco

11.30 p.m: bar closes

12.30 a.m: carriages

Timing is all

The following lists will help to gauge the amount of time needed during the day for the bride, the groom and at the venues. Just put a time before each task to get a picture of what the day will hold for you. (Not all of the items may be applicable to you.)

Bride's time list

_____ Wake up / breakfast

_____ Hair appointment

_____ Make-up appointment

_____ Bridal party / maid of honour arrives

_____ Arrival of flowers for bridal party

_____ Get dressed (approximately two hours before ceremony)

_____ Arrival of photographer

_____ Arrival of videographer

_____ Photo session begins

_____ Arrival of bridal car

_____ Leave for ceremony

Groom's time list

_____ Wake up / breakfast

_____ Florist arrives with boutonnieres and corsages

_____ Arrival of photographer

_____ Arrival of videographer

_____ Arrival of car for groom and ushers

_____ Leave for ceremony

Venue timing

_____ Arrival of florist to decorate the church / venue

_____ Arrival of musicians and soloist

_____ Ushers arrive to seat guests (usually $\frac{1}{2}$ – one hour prior to ceremony)

_____ Groom and best man arrive (usually 20 minutes prior to ceremony)

_____ Parents of the groom are seated (if not walking up the aisle)

_____ Bride's mother and father arrive

_____ Bride's mother is seated (after last guest is seated)

_____ Bride and bridesmaids arrive (five minutes prior to ceremony)

_____ Prelude begins

_____ Processional song

_____ Registry signing song

_____ Recessional song

_____ Photo session begins after ceremony

Reception timing

_____ Photo session at reception venue begins

_____ Guests arrive at reception location

_____ Canapés and drinks are served

_____ Receiving line is formed

_____ Bride, groom and bridal party are introduced

_____ Best man's or father's toast (these may take place after the meal)

_____ Response of the groom (this also may take place after the meal)

_____ Dinner begins

_____ Speeches

List the speakers in order of appearance by full name:

1.   2.

3.   4.

5.   6.

_____ Cake cutting

_____ Dancing and music to begin

_____ Last dance

_____ Departure of the couple / car pick-up

Tip

Don't get too hung up on timing — the list is only a useful guide. Being too regimental may spoil the day, although a structure is needed.

Contact list

Put company names and direct contact numbers on a list and hand it to those who are helping to arrange the day. Below is a sample list; you may wish to add others such as the best man (Wake up, it's show time! Where's the ring?).

Hilary Fleet — caterer: 01243 999 9999

Mick Fleet — in charge of staff: 01243 999 9999

John Mitchell — car hire: 01243 222 2222

Peter Jordan — musicians: 0789 111 3232

Lori Matthews — flowers: 01798 666 6666

Andy Bedford — photographer: 020 700 1111

Maurice Welford — keys to village hall: 07892 444 000

Jonathan Digby — lighting and staging: 0798 000 1111

Honeysuckle Weekley — cake: 01243 500 6060

Car hire itinerary

If you have a number of cars to organise don't leave it to the last minute to decide who is going in which car and where people are being picked up. Don't forget to make any changes to the list if people drop out or have other transport arrangements — this can lead to delays and even a frayed temper or two. Here are some sample car arrangements:

Pick-up 1

Car hire 1 — 6-seater: 11.15 a.m. sharp

Passengers (5 in total): bride, bridesmaids (3) and father of the bride

Location 1: from 27 New Park Road, Bath to Tollgate Registry office, 16 North Parade, Bath

Location 2: 12.15 p.m: bride and groom from Tollgate Registry office to The Manor Barn, East Wittering Lane, Delling, Bath

Pick-up 2

Car hire 2 — 8-seater: 11 a.m. sharp

Passengers (5 in total): mother of the bride, grandmothers (2) and grandfather (1)

Location 1: from 27 New Park Road, Bath to Tollgate Registry office, 16 North Parade, Bath

Location 2: 12.15 p.m: parents of the bride, grandmothers, grandfather, bridesmaids from Tollgate Registry office to The Manor Barn, East Wittering Lane, Delling, Bath

It is necessary to work out the logistics in full with hopefully few changes.

Tip

Be firm with those needing transport — they can't change who they travel with at the last moment as the transport pack of cards may collapse.

2 Planning your budget

Deciding who will pay

Few about-to-be-married couples have access to unlimited money for their wedding. Budgeting is crucially important when starting to plan your nuptials.

First, let's examine who will be paying for the wedding. Will it be you both, one partner, a parent or set of parents or other members of the family? Maybe a godparent might step in with the offer of partial funding.

Often these days the couple, rather than the parents of the bride, take on the finances of their wedding. Ask your parents or family members you are close to if they can contribute to the finances (they could, for example, set up an account and pay monthly into it). Or ask them if they can share the costs by paying for a specific part of the wedding — the catering, for example, or buying the wine and champagne, or the travel costs. Make sure you give them a ball park figure so that they know what they may be agreeing to.

The traditional list of who pays for what

This is an indication of how expenses have been shared in the past, but nowadays any help is gratefully received — and offered if possible. These traditional guidelines help to split the responsibilities.

Tip

Each family's financial means should be considered when dividing the costs.

The bride's family:

- all aspects of the reception (catering, flowers, drink, staff)
- announcements in the press
- stationery and printing costs

- bride's dress and accessories
- bridesmaid's dresses
- bride's transport to the wedding venue
- the wedding cake.

The groom's family:

- engagement and wedding rings
- marriage licence
- church or venue fees
- formal dress for men in the wedding party (best man, ushers)
- buttonholes for the wedding party
- presents for bridesmaids and ushers
- transport to and from the wedding venue
- wedding night hotel costs
- honeymoon.

Keeping costs down

As previously mentioned, the average cost of a wedding in Britain has now topped the £17,000 mark. Expectations are higher and costs of catering and venue hire have reached new heights.

Naturally, no couple wishes to start their married life with debts from their wedding but it is quite easy to over-extend – over-expend – and throw caution to the wind as it's 'only once in a lifetime'. However, having a budget and keeping an overall eye on expenses is essential for the next step in your lives together.

It is very possible to spend less and still have a memorable wedding. It is, after all, the people who count and not all the add-ons, those so-called 'must-haves', that have accumulated over the years, such as expensive limousines, favours given out to guests, expensive beauty treatments, elaborate decorations, expensive gifts for bridesmaids and pages and other items.

The golden rule is to plan a wedding you can realistically afford. This doesn't mean asking too many people to your wedding and then offering them cheap food and drink – your wedding would be memorable for all the wrong reasons!

There are many ways you can keep costs down. For example you can dispense with the toastmaster, or find musicians who have just started on the professional ladder but who play and sing like angels. Hunt around for less costly, but still quality, drink and, with this book to help you, do the catering yourself with the help of friends and family.

Tip

Sticking to the budget will not only be a source of satisfaction but will give all concerned a peaceful night's sleep.

Prepare a list of proposed expenses (there is an example on page 28). That way you can control and keep an eye on your costs. But do record any changes as, inevitably, you will change your priorities several times over.

Be prepared to negotiate with each other and others who have a say in the finances. By discussion, not argument, you will reduce stress and any bad feelings that threaten to erupt. Of course, wedding planning is hardly plain sailing but if approached with a sense of balance and reality, you can enjoy the ride.

What are the average amounts spent on each category? The average bride and groom spend approximately 40% of their total wedding budget on the caterer (food, cake, and alcohol), 3% on the facilities for the reception, 8% on flowers, 10% on entertainment, 14% on clothing, 7% on a photographer, 4% on invitations and other printed supplies, 4% on gifts, 2% on transportation, and 8% on miscellaneous items.

Tip

In order to keep track of your wedding budget, it's a good idea to open a designated wedding bank account and start paying in a regular sum each month, preferably by standing order or direct debit. All bills can be paid from this account.

Controlling the budget

- Pare the guest list down to suit the budget. You can only start planning your budget once you have decided on the number of guests.

- Get several quotes and choose your suppliers (car hire, food, drink, clothing, printing, entertainment) with care. Always keep quality as a priority.

- Negotiate with your suppliers: ask for discount.

- Choose a date out of season for less costly catering and venue.

- Always make sure that all quotes include VAT at the outset, not when the final bill comes in.

- Keep accurate records, and keep them up to date.

- Communication is all: talk to each other, and to others.

Cutting food and drink costs

- Contact your local catering college: students may like to hone their skills by preparing your food. Student waiters may also wish to put their skills into practice. If going down this route, simplicity is best when choosing a menu.

- Choose a buffet as it is cheaper than a three course meal. It also keeps staff costs down. Or choose to have excellent, varied finger food for the same reasons.

- Start stockpiling supermarket bargain wine — but make sure it is quality, not sheer quantity. Or, if you live in the south-east, go to France to buy your champagne or sparkling wine and wine as they tend to be cheaper.

- You could decide to have a cash bar (see Chapter 6 for more advice).

- Ask a good cake-maker in the family — or a friend — to make the cake. Offer to pay for the ingredients.

- Serve your wedding cake as the dessert by adding fresh berries and a quality ice cream.

Cutting general costs

- Why buy expensive white satin shoes if you will only wear them once?

- Have your dress made by a local dressmaker rather than buy it from an expensive bridal shop. Take them a picture of a dress from a bride's magazine that you like.

- Consider having your hair done at a reputable salon's 'model's night'.

- Have a make-up lesson at a department store or go to a local college for a student make-up session.

- Use a good photographer but specify the number of hours you will to employ them, and the pictures you require.

- Alternatively, buy a good camera and ask a trusted friend to take pictures. Or choose a friend with a good camera and a noted good eye for photography.

- Ask a friend who has an unusual car if they will drive you to the ceremony. Or, if you live close to where the ceremony is to take place, walk with your bridal party and guests. This is a lovely tradition from other centuries and cultures.

- Turn your wedding meal into a country house party by borrowing crockery in one colour theme and placing wild flowers (allowable ones!) and branches in old vases.

- Buy flowers that are in season.

- Recycle your flowers by moving them from the church or registry to the venue.

- Make your own place cards rather than have them printed. Ask an artistic friend or family member to take this task on. They will enjoy being part of the event — just offer to cover their costs.

- Call in favours and ask a DJ friend to organise the music, agreeing on the playlist.

- Organise your own entertainment — you could, for example, have a game of cricket.

> **Tip**
>
> Scrap the evening party to keep costs down and have a knees-up in the pub. Buy everyone a first drink, or a nominal number of bottles of champagne or sparkling wine.

Making your budget list

This includes catering, the venue and general expenses. You may be able to put a line through some of the items below right away if they are not what you want. It is, of course, perfectly possible to spend quite a little on your wedding by judicial pruning — and vice versa!

- announcements in the press
- the bride's wedding ring
- the groom's wedding ring
- wedding dress
- bride's shoes
- headdress and veil
- groom's clothing
- bridesmaid's dresses
- beauty treatments/hairdressing
- flowers: at church or civil office and venue
- flowers: buttonholes
- transport costs
- printing costs

- church or civil fees
- photography/ video recording
- catering
- cake
- drinks (pre-meal, with meal, after meal, toast)
- catering/waiting staff
- wedding venue
- marquee
- equipment (if hiring a village hall, for example tables, chairs, tablecloths, cutlery, glass, plates, etc)
- decorations
- entertainment (music, DJ, toastmaster, staging, lighting, sound system, PA system)
- hotel expenses for bride and groom, family if applicable
- bride's going-away outfit
- honeymoon costs
- wedding insurance
- other expenses (for example taking parents out for a thank you meal, paying for an unexpected hotel or taxi bill, gardening expenses if having a marquee in the garden, house cleaning).

Preparing your initial budget

This is a process which needs research and time. Make a list drawn from the points on the above list in order of priority and start your research by getting quotes and promises (a lent Rolls, a DJ friend offering his or her services, a cake being made for you). At the end of your research and compilation, you will know what you can and cannot afford. If you have been promised funding by family or friends as well as your own financing, put the initials of the person or persons concerned against an item with the amount promised.

Getting quotes

Getting a quote from a company differs from getting an estimate. A quote or quotation is a price – or service – given to you by the company and is legally binding if in writing. An estimate is just that, an estimation of what they can provide. They can invoice you with a differing final sum as it was an estimate, not a quote. In the eyes of the law you cannot challenge them in court.

But when drawing up your provisional budget, you will be obtaining estimates from various companies rather than quotes. You may also change your mind as to what you wish the company to provide (you may wish to change the order to 110 chairs rather than the 90 in the initial estimate, for example).

Points to consider

Always check through the estimate to see if you have asked each company for the same items, as a cheaper estimate may be less as it has fewer items. Make sure you are comparing like for like, with quality over inferior products.

Always check to see if VAT has been included. Some companies are rather sly about this and only add it on to the final bill to ensure your order. This VAT less bill may seem a cheaper option at the outset but it won't be when the final bill is submitted.

> ## Tip
> Confirm all bookings in writing and save a copy for your records.

Wedding insurance

The chart below gives an idea of what is on offer. The three columns are for different grades of cover. Contact an insurance broker or go online to discover the options and get a quote. Be sure, however, before you sign on the dotted line, that you understand all the small print.

Cancellation of wedding and/or reception	£9,000	£ 18,000	£30,000
Rearrangement of wedding and/or reception	£6,000	£13,000	£22,000
Wedding / ceremonial attire	£3,000	£6,000	£10,000
Wedding gifts	£3,000	£6,000	£10,000
Wedding rings, flowers, attendants' gifts and cake	£2,000	£4,000	£10,000
Wedding cars and transport	£1,500	£3,000	£5,000
Photographs and videos	£1,500	£3,000	£5,000
Failure of suppliers	£1,500	£3,000	£5,000
Essential document indemnity (for weddings abroad)	£250	£500	£1,000
Personal liability	£2,000,000	£2,000,000	£2,000,000
Personal accident	£20,000	£40,000	£40,000
Legal expenses	£5,000	£10,000	£20,000

3 Compiling the guest list

Wedding guest list

It's your wedding. With this, of course, come expectations from a variety of family and friends who might think they're in line for an invitation.

Weighing up who should be invited can be a minefield as both sides of the family need to be taken into consideration as well as old friends, mutual ones and work colleagues.

Of course you will include closest friends and immediate family on your list. You will also include people who have been and will continue to be important in your life, Decide who are friends and who are acquaintances.

Paring down the list can be a fraught time. You may feel guilty, and a lot of discussion and compromise is needed on both sides. Be brave! Remember: you can always have a party after your wedding for those not included. This can be a highly joyous, charged-with-emotion occasion which will bring other friends and family together to share in your happiness.

Who will you invite to your wedding? Naturally you want your wedding day to be one of the happiest of your lives; the bride and groom need to take a firm grip on expenses so that costs don't spiral out of control. The very first step is to look at the guest list and decide how many people to invite.

Obviously, the more guests, the more expensive it will be. Catering, size of venue, possibly marquee hire, staffing, even printing costs needing to be taken into consideration. The biggest expenses are the venue, catering and the alcohol. Unless you have unlimited access to a stuffed-full-of-money bank vault, keeping the guest list down is *the* way to keeping costs down. Be ruthless!

This chapter covers the following:

- How to pare down your guest list to suit your budget and venue.

- How to invite your guests: the printed invitation, suggested wording and reply.

- Additional stationery — possible needs.

- Your table plan.

- To receive or not to receive? The receiving line's pros and cons.

- Children at your wedding.

Tackling the list

How can you tackle the guest list? Here are some suggestions:

- Write down all possible names, leaving no one out. But write down those names of people who you actually *want* at the wedding.

- Return to this list, highlighting those who you might possibly want to attend.

- Go over the list again, circling those who you **really** want to attend.

- Move these people over to a semi-permanent list, and then delete those who you haven't got such strong bonds with or you haven't seen for quite some time.

- Do you now have the beginnings of a guest list? Add the numbers up. Take a figure such as £50 (this may be the cost per person for the catering, venue and staffing, for example) and multiply it by the number of people.

- Still quite a hefty number? There is no rule in the book that you have to invite most of your family members on both sides. It is your wedding. Nor do you have to issue an invitation to guests to bring a guest unless they are partners.

- Decide on a smaller wedding if the numbers, and therefore costs per head, are high. As mentioned above, invite others not on the list to a post wedding party. This can take place within a few weeks of the actual ceremony and could be a drinks party with finger food or a simple barbecue with music.

Cutting down the list

- Don't invite people out of obligation.

- Don't invite school friends you haven't seen for decades unless you wish to start up that friendship again, although maybe this isn't the occasion to do it.

- Don't invite people whose weddings you were invited to a while ago if you haven't kept up with them.

- There is no need to invite friends' and family's children unless you are close to them.

- You do not have to give single people a 'with guest' invitation.

But who is paying?

If you are paying for your wedding, you will have the final say on the guest list. However, if your parents are contributing to your wedding, you will have to consider their guest list too. But you can still be the prime arbiter on who is coming to your wedding by suggesting a fifty-fifty or forty-sixty split between your list and that of your parents.

Tip

If dealing with lists from several sources (yours, both sets of parents), stipulate a deadline for the lists. Once you have finalised the list, get full names, titles (Dr, Mrs, Ms, for example), addresses, email addresses and phone numbers. If you have all this information to hand you can use it if you need to contact them for any reason (such as asking 'Are you attending?' if they don't reply).

The invitations

Now that you've finalised the all-important list you will need to decide how to ask your guests to attend your wedding. As the invitation is the first thing they will see, your guests need to understand what kind of the wedding they have been invited to. Is it formal? A casual, informal gathering? A small, intimate wedding party? Or a large one stretching over most of the day and evening with a party and dancing into the small hours?

Wording is key when writing your invitation. How important is etiquette to you? Are you keen on the more formal approach or the 'Hey, gang, we're getting married' casual way? Whichever route you take it is crucial for your guests to understand *what* they have been invited to. It is also important to spell out *who* is invited. For example:

- Have they been invited for the reception only or for the ceremony and reception?

- Is the invitation for the guest only, or for a guest and their chosen guest, a couple with children, or just a couple? Write on the invitation *who* is invited, not 'you are invited.' This is too ambiguous and could cause confusion.

- It is good manners to send an invitation to the groom's parents and to the officiant and perhaps his or her partner, be he or she a member of the clergy or the registrar.

- Be specific: it will save you a lot of time, potential embarrassment and uncertainty. The last thing you want is for guests who have assumed too much to come to the wedding with several in tow to find that there is no table place for them or not enough food.

Quantity of invitations

You will need one per couple or family but, when ordering, add 10–15% extra in case you have to send out further invitations. Printing costs tend to be static: the initial cost is key, the numbers ordered of less importance. (You will have quotes from several printers and samples of their work.)

Tip

Always order extra invitations and envelopes as mistakes can happen.

Today, however, it is perfectly normal practice to send out invitations by email or orally but you do run the risk — if the latter — of confusion (time, place, who is invited).

Types of printing to consider

You may have thought you could get away with just the invitations. But, like the proverbial duck kicking its legs under the surface of the water, there's a lot else going on. There might be:

- Response cards. These are for people to fill in and return to you. They are generally for larger, more formal weddings.

- Evening invitations. As not everyone is invited to both ceremony and the reception or party afterwards, another type of printed invitation may be necessary to send out to those just coming for the reception or party.

- Menus. These can be hand-written rather than printed.

- Order of service.

- Thank you cards. These can also be hand-written for a more personal touch.

You may also wish to consider printed cake boxes (your names and date, for example).

Colours tend to be black and white or cream and white but there are no hard and fast rules.

> ## Tip
>
> A cost effective way of making invitations is to buy some ritzy type of paper from an upmarket paper shop and print them yourself. Just make sure the weight suits your printer. Buy a few sheets and try them out before investing in paper you may not be able to use.

When to order

You will need to proof-read and adjust any printing, So, ideally it is prudent to place your order between three and four weeks prior to sending them out. Invitations typically go out two months before the wedding, which gives people time to plan any travel arrangements and time off work if necessary. It also gives time for those who need accommodation to arrange it.

Information to include

- Date
- Time
- Place
- Venue
- Who is hosting the wedding
- Type of wedding (church or registry office, for example)
- Who to reply to: you may wish to ask guests to reply to the bride's parents' address, their email address or by phone. Or you may be managing the guest list so add these details

- Directions
- Presents (you may have a wedding list you would prefer your guests to choose from, for example).

Examples of possible invitations

Below are examples of invitations. Note that instead of 'request the pleasure of' you may wish for the more informal 'please join us' with subsequent changes to the wording below to fit ('Please join Saffron Leon and Jonathan Pepper to celebrate their marriage', for example).

Miss Saffron Leon and Mr Jonathan Pepper

request the pleasure of

....

at their marriage

at Chichester Registry Office, 31 North Street, Chichester, West Sussex PO19 2SS

on Friday, 29 February 2008

At 11 a.m.

and afterwards for lunch at

The Manor Barn, South Parade, South Wittering PO20 6XX

(Directions are enclosed. There is parking at the barn)

Please reply to:
Saffron Leon
12 Solent Avenue
Chichester
West Sussex PO19 1ZZ
Saffron101@langfordwoodland.co.uk

Or, for a wedding invitation from parents of the bride after the ceremony

Mr and Mrs Selby Leon

request the pleasure of

....

at a reception at The Manor Bar, South Parade, South Wittering PO20 6XX

on Friday, 29 February 2008

At 1 p.m.

following the marriage of their daughter Saffron

to Mr Jonathan Pepper

RSVP: 100 Emsworth Road, Aldsworthington, West Sussex PO20 6YY
01243 888 9999

Names on the invitation

Add in writing the name or names who you wish to invite. It could be just the one guest, or a couple, a couple with children of a combination in the family such as Aunt Sarah-Jane and Claudia. Or, depending on the circumstances, if they live quite independent lives, it may be protocol to send each person a personal invitation. They may not be joined at the hip.

Tip

Depending on your budget and how formal the invitation is you may like to include a reply card with a stamped addressed envelope. The wording could include 'would be delighted to attend' or 'regret but cannot attend,' and guests able to choose either answer.

You could use postcards to keep costs down.

Going informal and casual

You may go for a more casual approach simply because you are both informal people. Or you may be getting married the second time around and aim to be fuss-free. Other types of invitations which maybe suitable:

- bright or pastel colours

- more unusual fonts (but not too quirky: you still want your guests to be able to read the invitation)

- using photographs of yourselves

- including poems or a quotation

- personalising the cards by using watercolours, drawings or stencilling

- creating your own design on your computer or asking a graphic designer to come up with suggestions that reflect your interests and personalities.

One Dutch couple invited me to their wedding with a card they had made themselves. It was a picture of the two of them in an open-top car in bright colours, the directions were hand-painted and included the church and path to the reception. Delightful and unstuffy.

Tip

Remember to check that you have the right postage for your invitations. Guests will be less than pleased if they are charged for incorrect postage and it will save a lot of time, effort and sheer frustration if you spend time ensuring each invitation is correctly stamped.

Arranging the seating

You will need a seating plan for a sit-down dinner of several courses and also for a buffet, depending on how keen you are for formalities. I find that most wedding parties opt for a seating plan for both types of catering. (You will not need one for a finger buffet as these are stand-up affairs with several tables with a number of chairs placed strategically around the space for those unwilling or unable to stand for long periods of time.)

Place two seating plans by either side of the entrance to the reception on easels so that several people at one time can see where they are sitting. Put the guest' names alphabetically, and put their table number against their name. The number on each table of the plan should be easily seen; colour coding can be helpful too.

There are numerous different ways to identify the tables. You may wish to name them after your favourite places (Paris, Brighton, Snowdonia, Covent Garden) or where your guests have travelled from (South Africa, Scotland), or simply number them. You could choose fruit or herbs pineapple, mango, kiwi, rosemary, thyme or coriander are some suggestions. Favourite or famous restaurants are other possibilities (The Ritz, The Savoy, Momma Cherri's Soul Food Shack)

Decorating the tables

Decorate the tables with fruit and vegetables or herbs in little terracotta pots which guests are encouraged to take home with them. Never place a large, overflowing flower arrangement in the centre of your guests' tables as they won't be able to talk to the guests opposite — or even see them. A maximum height of 12—14 inches (30—25 cm) is a good rule of thumb when planning table decorations, particularly at round tables.

Avoid all-white flower decorations. It takes a whole lot more flowers if you do; a splash of colour goes a long way.

Use fresh fruit and vegetables. Pineapples and pomegranates, for example, add panache. Or use chillies and tomatoes in pots in high summer with foilage to create a different look.

Poinsettisa, evergreen, red ribbons and mini trees can be highly effective in winter.

For something completely different and poignant add pictures of past family members at family weddings to the table decoration. It creates a good talking point.

For winter or evening weddings, use candelabras which can be hired — thereby keeping floral costs down. Add floating candles to attractive bowls for added effect.

For a beach effect, fill attractive buckets with sand, scatter with shells and other seaside paraphernalia.

What do you do with your floral arrangements after the party? Contract a nursing home beforhand to see if they would like the flowers for their communal areas or ask guests to take them home with them.

Place cards

After people consult the seating plan they won't remember who they are sat next to; place cards are essential for your guests' smooth transition from looking at the seating plan to finding their table. You could hand make them, but be sure that the names are legible.

Table menus

Either have menus printed, or hand write them as clearly as possible. Check with your caterer for the correctly-named dish and its components, or make sure that the catering you are providing matches the wording on the menu. Guests will be rightly perplexed it says *Chicken chasseur with a white wine, cream and herb sauce* only to be served *Chicken with a saffron sauce*.

Don't over-elaborate. There is no need to put *Ayshire roast beef resting on a bed of spinach and a pool of red wine sauce* — the pretentiousness is overwhelming. State your dishes simply but if someone you know has made something, do credit them — for example *Leonie's Eton Mess with local strawberries*.

Tip

You only need two or three menus per table of ten.

Working out the venue layout

First of all, you need to know your chosen venue and its size before tackling the plan. You will also need to know the size of the tables (are they square, round, rectangular, in one long line?) and how many these tables can seat comfortably.

The shape of the room or marquee plays a major part in determining the arrangement of the tables. The tables' position can add to the atmosphere — or detract.

Tip

If there are too many tables in a small space or too few in a large space it can spoil a party.

It is advisable not to have too much space between tables as guests can feel a tad too apart from each other. It is essential, if you are using a caterer, to talk to them about the layout and to the hall hirer about how many tables and chairs will best fit into their venue. You want your guests to be comfortable and not too squeezed in — or made to feel as if they really are in a barn.

The number of people at each table is, of course, defined by your guest list. The type of chair is crucial; some are too big and take up too much space around a table. It could make a difference to you if you can seat eight rather than six around a table — too large a chair might make it impossible.

Also, bear in mind that waiting staff need to get to each place, and your guests will leave to go to the toilet, go out for a cigarette or to speak to someone at another table. You need sufficient space around each table for ease of access.

Check it out

- Don't think that a child will take up less space. They still need a chair — this equals one space.

- Round tables look more attractive than square ones.

- Long trestle tables, banquet-style, can give you more space. They also help to create an easier, more friendly atmosphere with more of a communal feeling.

- Guests seated at long tables also have more people they can talk to if the tables aren't too wide. If they are too wide then all is lost: they can only speak to the person on their left and on their right. If those people are engaged in conversation with others on their immediate left or right, that guest is isolated.

It is better to have fewer tables with more people on them than fewer tables with a handful of guests who may have nothing in common and soon tire of their companions.

Seating guests

You can encourage a good atmosphere, but not completely run it. It's up to your guests to play their part and help you celebrate your day. When deciding on the seating, the following points are worth considering:

- The jury is out whether you seat people who know one another together or those who are new to one another. I suggest you use a bit of psychology when seating various people; many guests may be keen to meet new people, others less gregarious.

- Avoid seating people together who you know don't get on.

- Try to match people, for example those who may have subjects in common or who you think will hit it off.

- Mix the sexes up.

- Don't sit all the elderly together: they will benefit from sitting next to other generations, and vice versa.

- Sit small children next to their parents.

> ## Tip
>
> If you have a number of children coming get some booster seats in rather than high chairs. You can use the chairs you have chosen, and the booster seats simply go on them. But check them out beforehand to see if they are suitable and safe.

Advantages and disadvantages of a top table

The top table, often rectangular in shape, at which the bridal party is seated, is a formal affair and not suited to all weddings. The bride, groom, sets of parents or the bride's parents, best man, bridesmaids and perhaps honoured guests, are on view to all guests.

This is a great advantage when it comes to speech-making and pictures but people at the top table can only speak to those on their immediate left or right. The two at the end are left out in the cold if their immediate neighbours are talking to someone else.

I would suggest the more usual European banquet style of seating. This means everyone has a more pleasurable time as they have people oppo-site to talk to as well as those on either side.

However, formality often wins the day — in which case here is a traditional layout.

The top table's traditional seating plan

Chief bridesmaid — groom's father — bride's mother — groom — bride — bride's father — groom's mother — best man.

But the pattern may shift if, for example, the bride's parents are divorced and remarried. Then you could do:

Bride's stepfather – chief bridesmaid – groom's father – bride's mother – groom – bride – bride's father – groom's mother – best man – bride's stepmother.

Plus, of course, the groom's parents and other key people.

This seating plan can be adapted to suit any possibilities. For example, a brother or sister can replace the father who may be absent. A favourite godparent may also be elevated to the top table. There are no hard and fast rules in today's society.

The receiving line

Although this may seem rather formal, a receiving line at the reception entry is an excellent opportunity to meet and greet all your guests. It gives those in the line a chance to meet everyone. However, it can be time-consuming, and at a less formal wedding you could choose to meet guests in a different way. If you choose the receiving line this is a guide to get you started (it will vary depending on parental availability). Keep it short to avoid a queue and keep the conversation to a minimum.

- bride's mother
- groom's mother
- groom's father
- bride's father
- bride
- groom
- head bridesmaid

Inviting children to your wedding

Some weddings are a happy mix of all ages, other more formal ones perhaps not including children. Of course it is entirely up to you which route you take and should you include them, here are some tips:

- **Invite children for part of the wedding.** If the party goes on late, children can become fractious. Make the timing clear in your invitation to the parents.

- **Food**: serve the same food to children as adults. This is what the rest of the world does; the Anglo-Saxon take on children's food at variance.

- **Seating**: some smaller children may prefer to sit with their parents. Older children often like a table of their own (supervised by parents).

- **Dressing-up box**: this will keep children amused with a clothes including long dresses and old family hats, fairy wings, cowboy outfits, funny hats and action hero costumes. You may have a whole lot of dressing up or you could hire costumes in.

- **Treasure hunt and other games**: ask friends or family members to organise a treasure hunt or have a set of trampolines or physical games such as a bouncy castle to keep children occupied and having a great time on your wedding day. Just make sure that children are kept an eye on and that they are discouraged from leaving the venue.

- **Face painting**: hire a face painter for the day to engage the children in some fun.

- **Create a crèche** if there are a number of small children, and hire a nanny.

Children and second weddings

If you are getting married for a second time, you may well want to involve your child. There are plenty of imaginative and exciting ways children can be involved, especially in the ceremonies. Having children from a previous relationship, whether the bride, the groom, or both, the question to address very early on is what the children will do on the wedding day. Whatever you do, don't leave this until the last moment.

If a child is reluctant to be involved in any activity, and there may be many reasons for this, respect their point of view. Never force a child's involvement. Gently remind them that their presence is of great importance and that will be enough if that's where they feel comfortable. Do make sure there is a photograph taken of all of you on the day.

The roles which come easily to mind are bridesmaids (for second marriages with older children), ring bearers (page boys), best man or chief bridesmaid, again for older children, flower girls, and ushers – and if everyone is willing there is a lot to be said for this.

Involving children

- Some children are shy and won't wish to be involved. Suggest a behind-the-scenes task to make them feel included.

- Ask older children to hand out the order of service in the church, for example.

- Children are happy to be given tasks before the wedding too like sticking stamps on the wedding invitations, being involved in 'choosing' the flowers, the wedding cake, some items of food and what to offer other children to drink.

4 Setting the stage: choosing, equipping and decorating your venue

You've come a long way! You have chosen your venue, worked on your budget after taking into consideration your expectations for your wedding, and decided on your guest list.

Now is the time to fine-tune your equipment hire for the venue, confirm the size of your marquee, if you are using one, and all other important requirements such as, the dance stage, bar, flowers, and other major items.

This chapter will deal with:

- marquee hire companies and what kinds of questions to ask them

- hiring village halls or barns

- furniture you may need and how to get quotes

- dealing with suppliers including florists, types of flowers and flower arrangements

- the all important seating plan.

Tip

To find out about marquee hire companies, equipment hire companies, village halls and other venues look in your local *Yellow Pages* either online or in the book. Google companies too as not all will be in the *Yellow Pages*; you may also be looking further afield than in your local area. Do ask friends and work colleagues for their recommendations too.

Choosing a marquee

Marquees offer a flexible and sizeable facility within which you can choose the features and design. This allows you to put your stamp on your marquee and allows freedom from the backdrop that already exists at a fixed venue such as a hotel. If you have the garden space there is nothing nicer for many people than being able to spend the day at home entertaining family and friends.

By going for the marquee option you almost inevitably gain far more control over proceedings, both on the day itself and during the all-important lead up to the day.

Families can be free from the restrictions which are so often imposed by fixed venues. These can often limit the timings of the event, the choice of caterer/florist etc, even down to how loud the band or disco is allowed to play (but invite the neighbours!). This way you can decide on all the details, not ones chosen for you.

Tip

Please bear in mind your neighbours, or, if in a village hall, others living in the area, when turning up volume. Ask the village hall's manager about restrictions. If there are any please abide by them.

The same applies to your neighbours if you're holding your wedding at home: the thump-thump-thump of the base notes late at night can turn quite sane neighbours into very angry ones. Either invite them or have the courtesy to phone or drop a note into explain what will be taking place. Be considerate.

Types of marquee

The marquee business has completely transformed itself in the past two decades. Forget boy scout brown marquees with guy ropes, the wind whistling around the space between grass and your legs. As corporations and weddings have both become much more classy affairs, marquee companies have flourished. The types and styles of marquees now available is simply startling.

You can choose from:

- basic marquees

- marquees attached to existing buildings, or free-standing ones

- canopies as extra cover

- marquees with reception areas, dance areas, cloakrooms

- any size and shape – from round to square to fashionable Chinese hat types which can be linked together for a village effect

- Bedouin tents evoking North Africa complete with wall coverings

- catering marquees.

There are different looks you can go for:

- classic: simple and unfussy

- lavish: the décor might include deep reds and purples with a night sky star cloth

- minimalist: with ivory and neutral colours

- winter: burgundies, reds, oranges, winter decorations including Christmas trees, atmospheric lighting

- magical: a Midsummer Night's Dream look

- contemporary: silver and linen are possible looks.

The interior might include the following:

- pleated coloured or printed lining

- wooden walls

- flooring from coconut matting flooring to solid timber tongue and grooved

- standard flooring following the contours of the ground; a suspended floor for undulating ground; flooring that can rise to a height of five metres

- parquet dance floors or acrylic white ones

- double-glazed French doors and glass walls

- panic-bar fire exit doors and emergency safety lighting for large marquees

- clear marquee roofs to see fireworks through

- chandeliers, uplighters, pin spots or starlight ceilings

- covered walkways from the marquee to toilets

- good heating, electrical supply and water supply.

Other marquee possibilities

If money is no object, some companies will offer to create a complete beach with 20 tonnes of sand and palm trees; split-level marquees for dining and dancing; fountain displays with streams and foliage; indoor or outdoor fireworks; water screens with back lighting; laser beams inside or out with 3D creations and fire flame effects up to 25 feet high.

But, for lesser mortals, a less is more approach is needed. Don't be seduced into sinking too much of your budget into fripperies that might cause discord. Although your wedding should be as attractive and stylish as possible, this can be achieved by other means.

You may not need the full works of reception area, cloakroom, main marquee, toilets, catering marquee and covered walkway. Depending on where it is sited, and if you have access to a kitchen to suit your catering needs, enough toilets and other space for presents, coats and for small children to run around in, a basic marquee might be enough.

Tip

An open-sided marquee for summer weddings is an attractive option. The material can be rolled down. If the weather turns.

The full works

The reception area

Ideally this should be the first space that guests encounter, thereby keeping them in suspense as to how the dining area will appear. The reception should be large enough to allow guests to mingle easily and for staff to be able to get around with trays of drinks. In particular this area should be large enough to accommodate all of your guests in case of rain – a factor often overlooked in the understandable quest to save money.

Consideration should also be given to easy access for guests to toilets/cloakroom facilities, as well as to the practicalities of caterers' access for drinks service.

The dining area

This is often one of the most visually spectacular areas of a marquee (depending on the budget). The combination of the table layouts, lighting and décor arguably offer the biggest opportunity for visual impact and the all important 'wow factor'.

Decisions have to be made as to whether it is best for the dance floor to be central to the dining area — where most guests will be close to the dancing action, or whether greater impact can be achieved by having the stage / dance floor at the end of the marquee.

Buffet tables, bar/s and viewing points have to be allowed for. The position of the top table and cake table are also important, as photo opportunities, speeches, the cutting of the cake and so on have to be considered.

The catering marquee

It is vitally important to get this right. After all, this is the command centre of your food and drink requirements. What is incorporated depends on what you are serving your guests. If you are catering for a three course meal you may need cookers, you will certainly need refrigeration, some form of water supply and trestle tables for food preparation. It also needs to be big enough for your staff to move around efficiently, for storage of all the plates, cutlery, tableware and bottles and for the rubbish collection.

It should be positioned sensibly so that your staff won't have to walk too far from catering marquee to tables and bar; ideally halfway down the marquee for easy access. It must also be sited close to any vehicle such as a van which might house your refrigeration and access to other vehicles which might be storing other catering equipment and food. Make sure it has its own entrance and exit.

If you don't require too much food preparation — for example if you have decided on a simple buffet or finger food reception, a smaller catering marquee will be sufficient. But do factor in space for equipment storage, food, its final preparation on trestle tables, drinks and rubbish. And position it well so that staff can manoeuvre food and drink around the marquee easily.

Reveals

These are another feature of modern marquee design, and are an excellent way of introducing an element of surprise and fun to your wedding reception. A reveal is actually a false wall that is easily removable to 'reveal' an area behind. The most popular one is to shield a band area/stage/dance floor or dining area from view until a given moment.

Typically the dance floor can be revealed by dropping the false wall after speeches, giving the band the signal to start playing. Alternatively the dining area can be revealed at the end of reception. Some upper-end marquee companies will be able to give you a quote.

Additional features

By positioning windows carefully marquee companies will maximise the natural views offered by the marquee site. They will also take into consideration the fact that it is either a daytime event or at night, when outside lighting can provide attractive illuminated views of the features outside.

Safety issues are also given careful consideration by marquee companies as emergency evacuation of a structure in the event of fire has to be possible with minimum difficulty. This is especially relevant when split-level dining designs are incorporated.

Toilets

Portable toilets are an essential requirement if your guest list is a sizeable one. Available as single toilet units or as trailer mounted multi loos, they can be hired in many guises including basic 'bog standard' single units, luxury trailers, disabled toilets and loos with baby changing facilities as well as bespoke toilets, designed specifically for the event location. There are also companies which provide CD players, pictures, white porcelain bowls and solid oak or mahogany wood panelling and other luxuries.

A rough rule-of-thumb guide is to allow one portable toilet per hundred guests attending the event but I suspect those who thought this one out were probably the same people in charge of toilet number cubicles for places such as the Barbican in London (women's queues are quite a feature of the concert hall). Go for two at least per hundred guests is my suggestion. Women often get a rough deal at theatres, club and weddings.

Behind the scenes

The requirement for plant and technical infrastructure (such as generators, toilets, heaters, skips, etc) is substantial for a facility large enough to support a wedding reception for a few hundred guests. The positions of equipment like generators, toilets, heaters, service areas, skips and so on. needs careful consideration to ensure convenient access for all the suppliers, as well as making sure they don't spoil the views from, and appearance of, the marquee for your guests. Make sure when talking to marquee companies that these points are addressed satisfactomily.

Marquee sizes and getting a quote

Below is a guide for marquees of differing sizes. It shows how many you will fit in for a finger food reception or a sit-down meal.

Length in metres	Finger food reception	Sit-down meal
6	36	29
9	54	43
12	72	57
15	90	72
18	108	86
21	126	100
24	144	115
30	180	144
36	216	172

Do bear in mind that these figures will vary as to the type and size of the tables and chairs chosen. The siting and size of the buffet and bar also have an impact on numbers fitting in comfortably.

Below I have outlined some 2008 costs from a medium-priced UK company. Rememeber to shop around for the best deal but also look at the quality. If you go for the cheapest quote you may be opting for a less good deal.

General

White marquee

Fully lined

Matting

Lighting

Tables

Gilt chairs

Dance floor

100 guests

Typical cost: £3,300.00 (+ VAT £3,877.50)

Summer wedding / garden party

Marquee

Matting

Chairs

Tables

Dancefloor

Lighting

100 guests

Typical cost: £1,400.00 (+ VAT £1,645.00)

Spring wedding

Marquee

Carpet

Chairs

Tables

Dancefloor

Lighting

300 guests

Heating

Typical cost: £14,000.00 (+VAT £16,450.00)

What to ask marquee hire companies

You will find many marquee companies in your area. Search for marquee companies on the internet to find out who they are, look in the *Yellow Pages* or ask friends and family who they recommend. Once you have narrowed down a few, call and ask the following:

- Can I decorate my marquee to match the theme of my wedding?

- Do you supply heating and lighting?

- What is included in the quote (flooring, carpeting, lining, lighting, furniture, heating, loos)?

- How much space will I require?

- Will you carry out a site visit?

- Is it possible to use a marquee in winter?

- When will the marquee be erected and dismantled?

- Will someone be at the venue on the day of the wedding?

- Can you supply testimonials from previous clients?

- What will the marquee cost roughly to hire?

Working with the marquee company

As you can imagine, there are many things to take into account when arranging a marquee wedding reception. Make sure you employ a company that is professional and accustomed to foreseeing potential problems early enough to have solutions ready. Good professional marquee companies will not just provide a service in isolation but will do a full consultation with their prospective clients. They will check to see if what you require is the correct specification and will do the job properly. The following are crucial to get right:

- **The table layout**. It should fit the space so that it isn't cramped. Nor should the marquee be so big that atmosphere is lost.

- **Check on delivery and collection and erection**. Your garden must not be damaged. Check on vehicle access and space.

- **The company should be flexible with numbers**. If numbers grow and you wish to change the table configuration, find out if it is possible and what the cut-off time might be (for example, two weeks before the wedding).

- **The company must check with the caterer** (you or a professional one) to ensure there is enough space both inside and outside the marquee. This means both the service/preparation area and the dining/bar areas within the main body of the marquee itself.

- **Get key suppliers to meet onsite early** on to ensure they are all working towards the same goals. This includes the marquee company, the heating and lighting companies if they are different from the marquee company, the caterer, the toilet hire company and any other key player you have employed.

- **The heating**. How efficient are the heaters and how much noise do they create? Inefficient, noisy heating systems can ruin a wedding. I speak from experience.

- **Electrics** are also crucial to get right. If a lot of electricity is required, a generator is a must. Insufficient power could create power surges and losses, plunging the marquee into darkness. I speak from experience here too.

- **Ensure you have the telephone numbers** of the marquee company to hand: if you have any problems before or on the day – or even after the event (dismantling the marquee hasn't happened when asked) – you will want to be able to contact them. There will often be a duty manager who can talk you through any difficulties, or they will come to give you help.

Other marquee tips

- Book your marquee early, particularly if you are planning a summer wedding. Many companies get booked up well in advance. Busy months are June, July, September and December.

- Don't count on the weather playing fair. Ensure there is sufficient space in the reception area for your guests, their coats, your presents and for staff to circulate.

- Make sure the flooring suits the ground. Coconut matting may be cheap but it plays havoc on uneven ground, and guests can be left staggering about in their high heels and going flying.

- Is there a water supply for the catering marquee?

- Are the toilets within easy access of the marquee or have they been hidden away for aesthetic reasons? Weigh up the pros and cons. Some marquee companies offer to put toilets inside the marquee so that guests, especially in wintery months and in the dark, won't have to go outside. But make sure the toilets are well positioned so that queues don't snake back into the main marquee.

- Noise: who will be affected by late night music?

- Give good directions to the marquee company (and any other supplier) so that precious time isn't lost — as well as tempers. Supply them with a map, times (putting up, taking down) and address with contact phone numbers. Get their mobile numbers.

- Set out details in writing. Have a contract.

Establishing your layout

Marquee hire companies will more often than not supply layout plans. It is a good idea to establish early on the likely numbers of guests for your wedding so that one can be drawn up. This is a highly useful tool when dealing with your potential suppliers. A good marquee supplier will draw scale diagrams of the marquee layout to make sure that you have the right sized one.

Points to take into consideration regarding the space:

- dining tables and chairs — round, square or long joined trestle tables?

- dance floor

- buffet tables

- bar or bars for a larger wedding

- stage for musicians

- cake table

- present tables

- coat hanging space

- well positioned entrance.

Tip

Marquee security is vital both before and after the wedding. Don't be tempted to put all your alcohol in the marquee as it could be stolen. This applies to anything of value, including presents, left overnight. Take out insurance and secure the marquee.

Factor in lighting paths. This can be forgotten, with the result the people have to find the toilets, the entrance to the venue or the way back to a car park in the dark, which creates accidents. Ask the marquee company for advice or light paths yourself. If choosing candles and other naked flames, make sure they are placed safely and don't create a fire hazard. Also bear in mind your guest list; children love to play with them.

Hiring a local venue

If you are planning a wedding in the country, you will have access to village halls or barns for hire, as well as other venues (see Chapter 1). If you live in a town or city there are similar halls which are for hire; cricket or bowls clubs or working men's clubs are possible venues.

You may have a lovely village hall available to book for your wedding but if not, do look at neighbouring villages. Ask friends and family for recommendations and contact parish councils to see what they may be able to offer.

When you have found a venue you like, ask questions (as outlined in Chapter 1) regarding costs, deposit, seating capacity, equipment, alcohol licence, the catering facilities and other essential information. Other things to remember are:

- Ask what time the venue will be available from so that you can decorate and set up chairs, tables and any other items.

- Visit the premises to see what the facilities are with a checklist. Chairs, tables and toilet facilities are of paramount importance.

- Check all the equipment which comes with the premises beforehand. Make sure that it is useable and clean. Are there enough plates, cutlery, glasses and other equipment? You don't want to have to find ten extra plates when serving the food.

- Ask about getting into the premises. Who will have the keys and who will you hand the keys to after you have tidied up after the wedding? Make sure you have a name and a mobile or landline phone contact number.

- Find out about rubbish disposal. Some venues ask you to remove all rubbish including bottles, others providing a rubbish removal service.

- Be firm about the cleanliness of the venue. Will all traces of previous users be removed? The last thing you want to do is to clean the place and remove rubbish before setting up your own wedding party.

- Some of the points mentioned in the marquee hire information above will be relevant to your village hall – such as size, layout and equipment. You may also wish to add a small marquee for extra space. Ask the village hall or barn manager if you can use adjacent space to erect a marquee or tent or to hire in extra toilets.

- Find out about parking: is there a car park? How many cars can it take? Or is there car parking in the area available for use by those who hire the premises?

Hiring catering equipment and furniture

You can find hire companies in the same way as the marquee companies: via the internet, *Yellow Pages* or by word of mouth. Give them a call or look on their website to narrow them down. Then visit several to see what they offer and if it is the type of equipment you would like to use. Do you like the cutlery, the glassware, the plates, the tablecloths?

There are two avenues open to you: to hire equipment which goes back clean (a cheaper method), or to hire equipment which goes back dirty. I suggest the latter as it is worth its weight in gold, especially if you are working in a marquee with no running water or in a small kitchen. With the best will in the world, washing up 100 first course, main course and dessert plates, plus hundreds of glasses and cutlery items, is beyond most people unless they have a dedicated team.

If working from a village hall you may find that the hall has sufficient plates, cutlery, glasses and serving dishes for your needs. But don't bank on it. When visiting the hall count all items as you may find – too late – that you don't have enough plates or cutlery. There may also be a combination of various sets given to the hall, or they may be inferior quality. If so you could think about hiring your own equipment.

Village hall kitchens are rarely updated to a high standard. There may be insufficient sink space and the water boiler often can't cope with a large party. Ask those in charge about the boiler capacity.

Equipment list

You may require the following:

- table linen
- napkins (or have paper ones)

- side plates

- main course plates

- dessert plates

- dessert bowls

- cutlery (teaspoons, small knives and forks, large knives and forks, dessert spoons and forks, bread or cheese knives)

- serving spoons and forks

- serving dishes, bowls and platters

- salad bowls

- salts and peppers

- bread baskets

- butter dishes

- sauceboats

- canapé dishes and serving plates

- tea cups and saucers

- coffee cups and saucers

- sugar bowls

- milk and cream jugs

- tea pots

- cafetieres

- highball glasses (good for beer, water and soft drinks)

- water glasses

- wine glasses (several sizes if serving white and red)

- champagne flutes or bowls

- water carafes

- bins (for rubbish and for cooling wine and beer)

- ashtrays.

You may also need the following:

- non-slip drinks trays

- water boilers

- plate stackers (tiered for a number of guests so that courses can be plated and put on hold on the stacker prior to serving an invaluable space saver)

- large pans, roasting tins

- industrial cookers, fridges, barbecues.

Tip

When calculating how many glasses, plates, for example, needed for the party, take into consideration, glasses for water, pre and post-dinner drinks, glasses for staff, musicians and others who may be at the party, such as drivers.

Furniture

You will obviously need chairs, tables and buffet tables. These can be either hired through the equipment company or from the marquee company. Bear in mind that large tables and chairs take up a lot of space. If space is at a premium whenever you are, choose less bulky tables and chairs (some tables for ten can seat eight, for example, with smaller types of chairs). Go the French wedding route and choose joined up trestle tables in long rows. They are more fun and inclusive and less formal.

Tip

Many equipment hire companies offer top-quality items such as:

- Villeroy & Boch presentation plates

- coloured glass water goblets

- coloured glass liner plates

- plain or cut crystal glassware

- speciality linen — velvet, brocade and textured fabrics

- chair covers — all the rage at the moment

- napkins tied with ribbon to match the décor.

Getting quotes

Once you have decided on your equipment hire company, ask them for a quote. Go through it very thoroughly and weed out items you think you may not need. At the same time add items you have left out — coffee spoons or salts and peppers for example.

Other things to check for are:

- delivery and collection dates

- who the invoice will be made out to. If someone else is paying, make sure both parties know

- any clauses regarding breakages and losses
- see if VAT is included. If it isn't clearly marked, you may be in for a big surprise when you get the final invoice.

Tip

Give the company good directions and a map if necessary.

There is rarely enough time to count all the items when setting up a party but, if you can ensure this is done, you will save yourself a lot of bother and possible expense if items are missing. Or your staff may only have the time at the end of the party when clearing away and stacking everything into their boxes to do a count, cross-checking the list which came with the order. Note the losses and breakages.

If you do have the time to check every item and find that some are broken, chipped, cracked or just missing, inform the hire company as soon as possible after the party. Also check each tablecloth. Some may have holes or tears or are stained. Don't get charged for these.

Tip

If you are using friends and family members as staff ask them to watch out when clearing food in the bin when emptying plates. It's so easy to discard cutlery with leftover food which you will have to pay the equipment hire company for replacements. This goes for some untrained staff too who may be too rushed as there may not be enough people to help with service. They may try to cut corners — with expensive results.

Tip

When clearing glasses make sure that those doing it know how to do so properly or breakages will occur. You will then be liable to replace all broken items.

Sorting out your seating plan

A good table plan is key to the success of any wedding. Without a table plan you risk an unseemly rush for the 'best' tables. Key guests end up seated on inappropriate tables, couples are split up and guests are still milling around when the food is being served. Conversely, a good table plan makes the whole seating process quicker and smoother. It also allows you to mix groups and families and to introduce new people.

But where do you start? First of all you should have already decided on:

- the number of guests you wish to attend your wedding
- the venue
- what shape of table the venue will use to host your wedding breakfast.

Knowing where you are going to have your wedding breakfast is important for deciding on your seating plan. The shape of the room will play a large part in determining the way in which the tables are arranged to best create a great atmosphere.

If the tables are spread too far apart your guests will feel very isolated at their tables. If you place the tables too close together guests will feel uneasy and not have any room to extend their chairs in order to visit the buffet, toilets, bar or to talk to other guests.

> **Tip**
>
> If you intend to have wedding entertainment during the meal, such as musicians or magicians, make sure you factor in the space as this may also impact on the way in which the tables are arranged in the room.

How to make a plan

The number of people you have at each table depends on how many guests you have, how many tables you have and how big the venue is. It is better to have fewer tables that are full, but not crowded, than many tables with only few people on each. If you have the luxury of space, try to give everybody enough elbow room to be comfortable.

To make a plan you will need:

- place cards
- markers
- notebooks
- pens
- rulers

Step 1:

Go through your acceptance list and make sure everyone is accounted for, including those who responded verbally and members of the wedding party, as well as their partners and children.

Step 2

List the names of couples and their small children in groups, so you can seat the family together. You may decide on a teen table. But don't seat all the elderly together: mix up society.

Step 3

If you are having a head or top table, list those who will sit there. You may wish their partners to sit at a nearby table.

Step 4

Draw a diagram of your reception venue, indicating the locations of the tables, the band or DJ, the cake, buffet tables and so forth. Keep in mind that elderly people or those with hearing problems probably won't enjoy sitting next to the speakers; pregnant women may want to be close to the toilets and disabled people will need access.

Step 5

Number the tables in a logical order so they'll be easy to locate.

Step 6

Write down each table number, followed by lines equal to the number of seats available at the table (usually eight or ten).

Step 7

List the names of everyone who will be given a particular table. Allocate people to tables rather than actual seats, as this system is easier for you and allows for friendly mingling. Or, if you wish for a more formal seating plan, allocate seats for each guest.

Step 8

Arrange for an extra table to accommodate those who respond at the last minute.

Step 9

Make signs bearing the number for each table and assign someone to place the signs as you have indicated on your diagram. Someone should be designated to have the diagram and the guest list in case there is a question. Compile a guest list with table number as a cross-reference.

Step 10

Prepare place cards for the head table and for all tables if you have decided on seating everyone.

Step 11

Make two large table plans and place them at the entrance to the dining area, placing them at a good height for all to see without having to bend over. Write clearly or print the names off in bold capitals and cut and paste. Check the seating plan by checking all the names off to make sure you have included everyone.

Tip

In this website-crazy world there is, of course, software for setting up a seating plan. www.perfecttableplan.com has so many bells and whistles that you'll be able to set up an entire banquet for the Queen and visiting dignitaries if you wish.

Planning flowers for your venue

Flowers are an important part of your wedding with many options open to you, roses, according to a poll, the most popular choice. How to choose your wedding flowers? Do you prefer a formal-looking bouquet of roses or a more casual posy of mixed flowers?

The choice is daunting when it comes to choosing which ones for church or registry office or venue. You may also wish you and your brides-maids, if going down this traditional route, to have bouquets or headdresses. Which colours, shapes and sizes will best suit the bride and the bridesmaids? What flowers are in season? You really need to consult a florist for these questions but do visit a number to find the right one for you. Many florists will offer the following:

- An initial consultation along with a quotation based upon the information given by you.

- A second consultation (nearer the wedding) to finalise arrangements.

- A meeting with you at your venue/reception to discuss and advise on your requirements.

- Delivery of the main Bridal party flowers to your specified address.

- Delivery and set up at your church/venue/reception.

Florists may also give a free bridal bouquet if you spend a certain sum on flowers, offer original flower designs and also the hire of decorative trees such as birches and vases.

Flower tips

Instead of paper confetti, a shower of flower petals is a most attractive ceremony send-off — and biodegradable.

Flowers have always been used for decoration at weddings. Bridal bouquets, buttonholes for men and table decorations are just some of their uses.

At one time the bride's flowers had to be white, but this no longer applies and any colour flowers can be used. The bride and bridesmaids usually carry bouquets or posies, and the bride may choose to wear one or more flowers in her hair or on her headdress.

Some people refer to the symbolic meaning of flowers when they choose flowers for their wedding. Orange blossom is one flower that has always been associated with weddings because it signifies purity and chastity.

A combination of red and white flowers is often avoided as they represent blood and bandages to some people.

Roses are a popular choice as they represent love while some people avoid peonies as they represent shame. Ivy symbolises eternal love.

The meanings of some flowers can differ between cultures. Lilies represent death to some people, while to others they indicate majesty. Some suggestions include choosing flowers which hold special memories or family significance.

The flowers you can use on your big day will also depend on the season.

Flowers at the church

When decorating a church you should first find out what the church's policy is.

Registry office flowers

If your ceremony will be at a registry office, it is also useful to find out what their floral policy is.

Reception flowers

Floral decorations for your reception might include a large display just inside the entrance and arrangements for each table. The wedding party table will feature a more ornate floral design.

Cake flowers

Flowers are a lovely fresh addition to wedding cakes and are an attractive alternative to traditional bride and groom figures. Flowers which sit flat such as gerberas look particularly effective.

If you wish to do your own flowers, here are some tips on seasonal ones and which flowers go with others.

Seasonal flower availability and arranging

Tulips are available from December to May with the main supply between January and April. Holland is the main breeder but tulips are also grown in the UK. They are available in every colour except blue and there are many varieties, including single, double, parrot or lily tulips. Tulips look beautiful on their own, but they also look excellent in an arrangement with other spring plants.

Hyacinths are available from November to April and are grown in the UK and Holland. Striking hyacinths impress on their own or with foliage and other spring flowers.

Syringa is grown in Holland and available from November to May. Syringa looks good accompanied with roses or lilies. A large bunch on their own is also effective.

Lilies are available all year round, and are grown in Spain, South Africa, Holland and the UK. Stunning enough to be used alone, they also work well as a focal point for a large arrangement.

Roses come in a range of colours, except blue. They are available all year round and are grown in countries such as Holland, Kenya, Zimbabwe, Israel and the UK. Roses look beautiful in any arrangement. Try them in a simple vase with a limonium and don't be afraid to experiment with the many different colours and shapes available.

Freesias are available in the UK, particularly in the Channel Islands and Holland. They are available all year round. Freesias add fragrance to any arrangement, but they are also delightful on their own or with foliage. They also work well with roses.

Stocks are most plentiful in May and September, but they can be found almost all year round. The main sources of supply are the UK and Holland in the summer and Israel and Kenya in the winter. Striking enough to hold their own in a large arrangement, Stocks also work well with foliage or on their own.

Agapanthus The main season is June to August but it can also be found in November and December. It is mainly cultivated in Holland. Use the long stems and large flower heads of the agapanthus to your advantage by using them on their own in a striking arrangement. They are also able to stand their ground in larger arrangements.

Ornithogalum is available all year round, but the peak period is from July to October. It is mainly supplied by Holland, the Channel Islands, Spain, Kenya and South Africa. Star-shaped flowers work well in arrangements with other star-shaped flowers. Go for contrasting colours and textures.

Sunflowers are plentiful from July to October when they are grown in the UK and Holland. They are also available at other times of the year from Israel and Spain. Sunflowers can be arranged simply in a tall vase. They also look stunning in large arrangements, or with natural green foliage and flowers.

Protea The main countries to supply the protea are Australia and South Africa. They are available all year round. Proteas are large flowers with heavy stems, so they need a sturdy container. Arrange them on their own with a small amount of foliage.

Ranunculus The main season is January to May. They are cultivated in Italy, France, Holland and the UK. Ranunculi arranged in mixed colours look impressive — but so do single colours combined with other flowers, such as tulips.

Allium Grown in Holland, Israel, France and Kenya, alliums are available as cut flowers between January and August in a range of colours including blue, pink, yellow and white. The tall stems of Allium giganteum look spectacular on their own in a large, glass vase.

Strelitzia They are available all year round and are grown in their native South America, the Canary Islands and Sri Lanka. These flowers can be displayed on their own in a tall sturdy container, and they are excellent for display work. The large, leathery leaves are also useful for foliage.

Lisianthus Available all year round, in the winter the main supplier is Kenya and the rest of the year they come from Holland and the UK. They look good on their own in a tall vase or with green foliage.

Alstroemeria is available all year round in a wide range of single and variegated colours. Use this flower to add colour to mixed arrangements. It also looks superb on its own or in a vase with some foliage.

Bloom Chrysanthemums are available all year. The single bloom or standard chrysanthemums have one bloom on each stem. They are usually the larger types of chrysanthemum, and are available in a range of colours from white and gold through to red. Try arranging chrysanthemums with seasonal foliage.

Delphiniums Originally just blue, delphiniums now come in shades of pink, lilac and white. The main source of supply is the UK, Holland and Spain. Display delphiniums on their own or with other flowers of similar colouring or shape.

Oriental Lilies Today, the main sources of supply of oriental lilies are the UK, Holland and Spain. They are available all year round, but are more abundant in summer and early autumn. Single blooms or several blooms displayed in a tall vase look very effective. They can also be combined with other flowers or foliage.

Amaryllis is mostly available from October to April, and is grown in Holland. On their own or with a small amount of foliage these flowers always look dramatic.

Anemones season is from November to May, they are produced on the Mediterranean coasts of Italy and France, as well as Holland, and the UK. Mix anemones with other flowers or use them in either single or mixed colours to make beautiful posies.

(Flower tips courtesy of flowers24hours.co.uk and weddings.co.uk)

5 Planning the entertainment for your wedding

One of the highlights of any wedding is the entertainment at the reception. Music in particular puts guests in the mood for a party and creates an air of celebration. This chapter covers music and musicians and other various types of entertainment you may wish to consider, such as fireworks.

Photography and videography are also covered here as well as the advantages of having a toastmaster.

You may wish to have traditional entertainment at your wedding: a band, DJ, or recorded music. But you could also explore some other ideas, depending on your budget and natural leanings. You may wish to do some research into having one or two of the following types of entertainment at your wedding:

Entertainment possibilities

- acrobats
- bagpipe players
- balloon rides
- barn dance and caller
- bouzouki (Greek) band
- calypso
- camel racing!
- coconut shies
- dodgems
- face painters
- fruit machines
- fortune tellers

- guitarists

- indoor fireworks

- harpists

- jesters

- juke boxes

- magicians

- rhythm and blues band

- tarot readers.

There are many other types of entertainment too. You could engage one of the groups of singers who dress up to look like waiting or other staff, only to sing at different tables rather than on stage.

If you do engage any acts, make sure you get a contract or a written statement which should include their intended playing time, or numbers of acts the company will perform, and their charges in full including any travel or other expenses.

Tip

Ask friends and family for recommended acts. You will be surprised how many of them will have some ideas.

Deciding on music

There are so many different types of music, from classical guitar and harp to full big band and country and western or jazz, that you might find the choice quite daunting. On the other hand you may have a clear view of what kind you would like at your wedding, be it singers, a single violin playing in the church followed by a Jewish klezmer band, or good old-fashioned rock and roll after the meal and speeches.

You don't have to have a 20-piece band to make your party go with a swing; it's up to you what music you choose to set the atmosphere. Don't, however, choose only the kind of music you personally like (rap won't go down too well with the majority of your guests!). Choose music which will give a sense of occasion and joy; music to dance or listen to. Remember that your neighbours may not like the decibels cranked up to full volume late at night if you are having your reception at home or in a built-up area. Inviting the neighbours is one way to get around this.

Hiring musicians

When narrowing down your preferred type of music, ask those musicians who you have contacted to send a demo tape or CD. Most bands have them.

Some useful questions you may wish to ask:

- Are you free on the day?
- Do you have a song list?
- Can you play the special songs we would like to have?
- Can you take requests from guests?
- What age groups do you play for?
- How many musicians and singers will perform?
- Which instruments do you use?
- How long has the group been performing at weddings?

- Do you supply the staging and lighting?

- Do you require extra power for your equipment?

- What are your rates per session?

- Does this include any extras (VAT, travel, meals)?

- What do you charge for overtime?

- Do you require a deposit?

- How many sets do you play and how many rest breaks do you take?

- What is your cancellation policy if the wedding has to be postponed or called off?

- Can you provide testimonials?

Be clear on what you expect. Check the set-up time, when you would like the music, the type of music (fast or slow), and inform musicians of the order of the day so they don't arrive too early — or too late. Get a contract and check the details.

Tip

Contact the local symphony orchestra if you prefer classical music. Many musicialns earn extra money by working at weddings.

Hiring a dance band or musical group

Book a band as early as possible, especially if you have chosen a popular time of the year to get married. Saturday bookings in particular get snapped up.

- Hire a three-piece band for small weddings of fewer than 75 guests, a five-piece band for guests of 100 or more, a seven-piece band for weddings of 200 plus.

- Bear in mind the space you will be using for the music. A small space with a big band or loud music will cause conversation to stop — not all guests appreciate loud music.

- Bear in mind also your guest list (ages, musical preferences).

Hiring a disc jockey

Music at weddings can vary according to the time of day or night. You may wish to have live dance music or a single harpist, or you may decide to have a DJ for the party after the meal. A good DJ is better than an indifferent band if he or she chooses a varied style of music. Some advantages of a quality DJ are:

- they choose well-known songs by original artists, and will liaise with you about when you would like some songs or other music to be played;

- they take fewer breaks than bands, so the music is more continuous;

- they can provide background music for the pre-meal drinks and dinner before launching into dance music. Of course, bands can play prior to the dancing but they tend to dominate rather than play more unobtrusively.

DJ hire tips

When choosing your disc jockey try to do the following:

- Ask your friends for recommendations and find out about the DJ's personality.

- Ask potential DJs for their play list.

- Avoid ones with overbearing personalities and crass jokes.

- Find out if he or she uses fade mixing (starting the next song as the one being played is faded out), beat mixing (blending two songs that have similar beats and tempos to create a seamless transition from one song to the next), playback medium (compact discs, minidisks, cassette tapes, records, or a combination) or other methods.

- Find out about the equipment used: the better the sound system, the better the reproduction.

> ## Tips
>
> Ask your band or DJ how long it will take them to set up and if they need any equipment or special plugs or cables.

Photography and videography

Good photography can enhance memories of your wedding for years to come. However, some couples decide that photography and videography are unnecessary luxuries. If you do decide to have either, or both, you will need to get quotes from companies or individual professionals for the following:

- cover fee

- per hour fee

- album fee

- duplicate album fee

- extras

- if videography has music incorporated in the package deal.

Questions for the photographer:

- Are you free on the day?
- Do you specialise in traditional or contemporary wedding photography?
- Can we see your portfolio?
- What type of camera do you use (digital, film)?
- How many hours do you suggest – and why?
- What is the cost for additional hours?
- Do you charge for travel time?
- Is VAT included in your quote?
- When can we see the first proofs?
- How much do you charge for albums?
- Can the pictures be put on a website for guests to download or buy?

Photographers can provide discs, do collages and graphistudio work, where wedding pictures are printed directly onto book pages with stunning results.

Digital photography is another suggestion: pictures are taken by one or several photographers with digital cameras, and the results put on your own website so that guests can download pictures and have their chosen ones printed off or sent on to friends and family. You can also create your own personalised wedding website.

> **Tip**
>
> Place disposable cameras on guests' tables — they can take more candid and informal shots which add a further memorable record of your day.

Videoing the wedding

Sometimes you will want a recording of your big day. Perhaps, for example, you have family or friends who can't be there.

There are different levels you can go to when filming, and you need to decide what you want. Do you want it simply of the service — with no intrusion — or more? It is up to you how far you want it to go, but be aware that too much can be a distraction and an irritation.

Toastmaster

Toastmasters are both men and women and often part of a guild of Toastmasters. They can add a real sense of occasion. The Toastmaster's duties include the following:

- Meeting with the bride and bridegroom approximately two months before the wedding in time to discuss their requirements.

- Giving helpful hints for those who are to make speeches, as well as hints and tips for the bride and bridegroom.

- Arriving at the venue early on the wedding day for a thorough check of all the arrangements on behalf of the host and hostess.

- Greeting the bride and bridegroom, parents and guests on arrival at reception and guiding them to the reception drinks.

- Giving discreet assistance to the bride and bridegroom, the parents, guests and photographer during the reception.

- Arranging for all guests to be introduced to the bride and bridegroom and their parents in the receiving line.

- Announcing and starting the applause for the top table for the wedding breakfast.

- Announcing and leading in the Bride and Bridegroom to applause.

Other toastmaster duties

Depending on the skill and type of toastmaster they may also make other required announcements, keep a watchful eye on everyone during the wedding breakfast and deal discreetly with any matters that may require attention.

They can also guide the bride and groom through the tradition of the cutting of the cake, announce the speakers in correct order and time-honoured fashion, assist the bride and groom with the presentation of their gifts and, at the appropriate time, provide a suitable conclusion to the wedding breakfast.

If it is a civil ceremony they can also be available to assist and guide the wedding party and guests immediately prior to and after the formalities of the ceremony.

If you search on the internet for 'toastmaster UK' you will find many companies specialising in this service. Contact them for details and costs.

6 Planning the menu

Deciding on your caterer or planning the catering yourself with friends, family and some professional help, is the next step. Will your budget, which you will have worked out by now, be able to accommodate a caterer or will you take on the challenge?

The first point must be how many guests you will invite to your wedding. If it is too daunting a task to contemplate cooking for 100 – or even 30 – then finding a caterer is the next step.

This chapter includes:

- choosing your caterer

- assessing your and your helpers' abilities as caterers

- deciding between a sit-down several course meal, or a buffet or a finger buffet

- weighing up other options: the champagne tea party; innovative catering

- selecting a menu: foods that go together and those that don't

- the wedding cake – make or buy? Alternatives to the traditional cake.

Choosing your caterer

When choosing a caterer to take care of your wedding food and drink you'll want to make sure you track down someone reliable and professional. Plan ahead and aim to meet caterers as soon as possible after deciding on the wedding date. If you have a venue which only deals with dedicated caterers, ask them for a list and contact friends or colleagues who have recently married for advice. But do remember that your tastes and expectations may vary from theirs.

Once you have a list of a few recommended caterers, set up face-to-face interviews to determine the right choice for you. Try to schedule a tasting as part of the interview. Your final decision should be based on taste, presentation and creativity, cost and the willingness of the caterer to suit your needs.

Qualifications

Although not essential, you might like to find out what qualifications and training the caterer has, and ask to see the certificates. But a word of common sense: not all caterers have qualifications, and many gifted amateurs have started up their business with nothing but creativity and flair on their side. Some qualifications are meaningless.

Insurance

Check whether the caterer has insurance, and if they do, find out exactly what type of things the insurance covers.

Fresh food

You want the food served at your celebration to be as fresh as possible, so ask the catering firm whether they use fresh food and produce. Ask them about the quality of their sourcing: do they buy free-range chicken for example? Some caterers use frozen or canned foods. If they do, don't take them on. The best caterers make everything from scratch using good quality, well-sourced food and cook with flair and imagination.

Portions

If you're planning a formal sit-down meal then it's important to find out the size of the portions, particularly if you've got salmon or steak on the menu. It's also worth checking the portions for a buffet. For example, it is very difficult to make sure that vegetarian dishes going only to vege-tarians in a buffet. Ask the caterer to do more portions as guests often try a little of everything.

Taste testing

Some caterers hold taste testing sessions. You want your guests to have a meal to remember — for all the right reasons — so ask to try some of the food of those caterers you have narrowed down.

Health inspected kitchen

It is vital that you make sure your caterer prepares the food in a health inspected and approved commercial kitchen. Many caterers start small catering companies from their home with no approved or inspected kitchen. To ensure the food you eat is safe you may like to hire a caterer who uses a commercial kitchen *unless* you have glowing reports from satisfied customers who use one-man band operations and who are professional to their fingertips.

> **Tip**
>
> Beware of caterers whose menus are relentlessly carbohydrate-led with a plethora of sausage rolls, pastry-laden food, breads and other 'beige food'. This is very cheap catering with little freshness, imagination, colour and texture to the food and one way of making a proposterously high profit. Choose caterers who cook fresh, perhaps local food, and offer lots of protein such as chicken and fish rather than potatoes and quiches.

During your consultation, ask the caterer to give an outline highlighting the cost per person, menu selections, service options and any additional fees that could be incurred. Come prepared with a list of questions you need answered, including:

- How long have you been in business?
- Do you specialise in a particular type of food and service?
- Are you familiar with the reception venue?
- What is your average price range?
- Do you provide rental equipment, such as linen and dinnerware? Ask to see samples.

- What is the ratio of waiting staff to guests?
- Where will the food be prepared? Will it be fresh, with local ingredients?
- Do you also provide wedding cakes?
- Are you available on the day of my wedding? Do you have any other events scheduled for the same day or time?
- Could I get a list of references from your previous clients?

Caterers will ask you the following:

- the date
- the number of guests
- the preferred time for the reception
- your catering budget per person
- the type of service required: a buffet? Sit-down meal? Finger food reception?
- delivery of food only, or setting up and serving?
- staff requirements
- alcohol requirements.

Signing the catering contract

Before signing a contract, read the terms carefully to verify the agreed-upon details. Be prepared to submit a 50% non-refundable deposit at the time of the signing, and make sure the contract includes the final balance amount and due date as well as the cancellation and refund policy. The contract should also include the caterer's contact information, the reception date, time, duration and location (including the exact name of the room, if necessary). Other details that should be outlined on the contract are the meal plan, type of service and staff provided, the cake and drinks.

Taking on the catering yourself

This does not have to be all your own work it can be a combination of family or friends who will help you cook the dishes you want on your menu.

If you are having a small wedding for, say, 30 people, you may wish to cut the costs and prepare the food yourself or with others. I will outline some of easy-to-prepare dishes in Chapter 7 – the kind of dishes that can be prepared in advance and served by either friends, family or hired staff.

Points to take into consideration if catering for your wedding:

- Do you have the necessary time to prepare freshly-made food?

- Do you like cooking? If you view the catering with a sinking heart, this task is not for you.

- Do you have a good back-up team in the shape of family and friends who are reliable, can cook, are happy to give their time and are committed to your wedding menu?

- Do you have a kitchen suitable for preparing food for a number of people? (It doesn't have to be a big one, just one which has sufficient counter space, fridge space and perhaps freezer space.)

- Are you a very organised person? Can you manage a team of friends and family?

Very simple food is the key to success: make the best cold roast beef, the best potato salad, the best green salad with croutons and homemade vinaigrette, the best vegetarian Thai salad with or without prawns, the best breads, cheeses, fruit salad. Notice the link? All cold food prepared in advance and dished up easily, without fuss.

> ## Tip
>
> Many amateur cooks tend to over-complicate menus and start cooking for the freezer as soon as the wedding day is announced. Why? By choosing simple dishes, the food can all be prepared within three days of the event. The outcome a far tastier, fresh meal. Keep it simple in every way. Panic not!

Will you be preparing a buffet, a two or three course meal or a finger buffet? Check out the pros and cons of these types of menus.

Buffet

A buffet can simply be a choice of three dishes plus one or two vegetarian ones, a selection of breads, cheeses and a dessert. Keep it simple by doing one dessert plus the cake or simply use the cake, as your dessert, adding fresh fruit, berries, cream or ice cream when serving it.

Pros: Buffets score as they keep down costs. A three course meal requires more staff and more kitchen space while a buffet offers two courses only, the main course and dessert. Dishes can be prepared in advance, can all be cold with, for example, the addition of hot new potatoes, and can be a great variety of flavours and textures.

Cons: Your guests might have to queue for their food for a long time if the buffet isn't managed properly. This can be dealt with effectively by having several 'stations' serving the same food. You may also have problems with guests not getting their fair share if some of the more popular dishes run out. When compiling a buffet menu it is advisable to identify those dishes that will be more popular and make greater quantities.

Sit-down lunch or dinner

This type of meal can be a more elaborate affair of two, three, four or even five courses (including a soup, a fish course, meat course, dessert and cheese). Then there's the cake. This is usually catered for rather than done yourself — those who do their own catering usually opt for a two or three course meal. For simplicity, I would suggest two courses with the cake, adding berries and cream.

Pros: All your guests are seated and are served the same food.

Cons: This can be more costly. Menus for a sit-down meal tend to have more expensive ingredients such as fish fillets and cuts of meats such as beef fillet or free-range chicken breasts. Hosts often feel that, as their guests are seated, they need to offer them a three-course meal. Waiting staff costs increase as you need staff to serve, clear and pour drinks.

Finger food reception

This type of reception is a clear winner for those who are on a tight budget and who don't wish to spend time and money on more elaborate buffets and sit-down meals. It is also a winner when it comes to entertaining a lot of guests as there is no need for tables and chairs for all, just a few for those guests who can't stand for long.

The food can be a mix of hot and cold bite-sized concoctions made in advance and simply re-heated if required, or served cold or at room temperature. The sky's the limit with the array of food you can offer your guests, from Chinese, Thai, Malaysian and Japanese to Italian, Spanish, Moroccan, British and French.

Pros: Platters of food are handed around with drinks, and the party lasting rarely over three hours. Staff are kept to a minimum. Little is spent on hiring chairs, tables, plates and other equipment.

Cons: Unless the food is handled well, it can be a disaster as some guests may not get any food if they are ignored by amateur staff who only serve those closest to the kitchen exit. The food must be of high quality, not the 'beige food' I mentioned before. As it is a celebration, the food must reflect this. Check your guest list: if you have many elderly people coming they will not appreciate standing for any length of time.

Champagne tea party

I don't know why more couples don't think of doing this ritzy, simple style of reception. The mix is easy: champagne in tall flutes, teas of various kinds served in smart china cups, cakes, sandwiches and cold finger food served on trays or tiered stands. Live music can add sophistication to the wedding party. It is easy to prepare and different from the usual type of wedding reception. It is casual but smart at the same time and allows your guests to circulate. Your guests will remember your wedding reception as being something out of the ordinary and ultra-cool.

It can be in or out of doors, and your guests can be asked to dress appropriately in cocktail dresses and black tie. This type of party can last anywhere between two and five hours in the afternoon or early evening. Just make sure the trays or tiered stands are replenished regularly to soak up the champagne. Tea is a very welcome addition to a reception from the start as it encourages guests not to over-drink, and caters for different ages.

Pros: You will keep costs down by not having to hire chairs, tables, plates, cutlery and other equipment. All the food can be prepared in advance, and you will need fewer staff. Live music — jazz, smooth Frank Sinatra-type, light classics or from the musicals — is a must to add an extra layer of atmosphere to your wedding reception, and your guests can dance. You can consider having more guests as costs are quite low despite the champagne or sparkling wine. (But make sure it's good quality whatever you choose to buy.)

Cons: There aren't many! Apart from some guests not being able to stand for long, in which case you may like to have small round tables with chairs scattered about the venue or garden to make your guests more comfortable.

Party 'stations'

Club Med, the French holiday company, hit on a great idea to serve their guests food. At many of their holiday destinations they group different types of food in a food court, and guests can choose different styles of food from all over the world. You could offer some of the following, each served at different 'stations':

- tapas
- fish and chips
- BBQ ribs and burgers
- hog roast
- curries and rice
- Chinese dishes with noodles, served in appropriate bowls
- cookie, brownie and pancake American stall
- chocolate in all its glories.

Pros: Guests choose their own food. The variety is appealing, and the mood one of fun.

Cons: You will need a lot of organising for this one and good staff to man the stations. You may wish to tackle it by finding a caterer who specialises in this type of catering.

Successful food combinations

When creating a menu Nico Ladenis, famed London chef-restaurateur, believes that 'perfection is the result of simplicity'. How true. Keep it simple. Culinary marriages made in heaven include:

- duck and orange

- salmon and sorrel or lemon

- strawberries and cream

- chicken with tarragon

- cold lobster and real mayonnaise

- lamb and garlic

- free-range chicken and mushrooms

- tiger prawns with Thai flavourings

- lamb and couscous

- roasted Mediterranean vegetables with goat's cheese or buffalo mozzarella

- the best breads and cheeses.

He believes, and I agree, that there should be no marriages between meat and shellfish or fish. Some dishes with fruit and alcohol also get the thumbs down — such as beef with Cointreau and mango!

Even simplicity demands care and attention to detail. Just throwing a whole lot of good ingredients together without the knowledge of food marriages will result in a mishmash of tastes and ill-judged flavours.

When deciding on what to put on your menu think about these guidelines.

- Don't choose two pastry dishes for one menu.

- Cook what you feel comfortable with.

- Avoid over-elaborate dishes that need a lot of work.

- Don't over-garnish your food. It just adds clutter to the plate and is time-consuming. Keep it simple.

- Track down good produce: go for free-range chicken, good local produce, the best breads and butter.

- Go for good chocolate with high cocoa solids.

- Source good wine and coffee or tea, not just the cheapest.

- Taste, taste, taste the products you buy where possible. If not, buy a minimum amount and cook it at home before buying in bulk. It may look good but could be a bad buy.

- Look at the balance of your menu, particularly if you're doing a buffet: are there too many cheese dishes? Too many of the same coloured dishes (brown, brown and brown)? Too many with dairy produce? Too much fried food? Too many carbohydrates (pasta, potatoes, pulses, rice)?

- Can you obtain all the ingredients when you want to cook them or will you be paying a premium if buying expensive South American asparagus in winter or raspberries from California in spring?

- Can you prepare all the dishes easily from scratch. Will they be fresh the week, or several days before, the wedding?

Tip

When narrowing down dishes for your menu, think about the amount of time it may take to prepare each dish. If something is too time-consuming you will regret having put it on the menu.

Looking after your staff

It is essential to remember that your staff need to eat too, especially if your party is a long one. You may wish to offer them the same food as you are giving your guests, in which case factor this in when counting heads before buying the food. Or, if your reception is a short one, make sure you at least buy some good sandwiches for them as they need food for energy and may not have eaten for several hours or longer. Inform your staff of the food arrangements for them. They will appreciate your thoughtfulness.

If you don't offer them food they will most probably help themselves and thereby create problems with the amount of food prepared for your guests. It happens! Treat them well and they will respond in kind.

The wedding cake

Most people wish to have a wedding cake, and usually choose the traditional tiered kind with fruitcake and marzipan. Others find this type too rich and sickly and opt for a sponge with icing only. You may be fortunate enough to have a family member make one for you (if so, present the baker with a bouquet of flowers at the cake-cutting) or you may wish to find a specialist cake maker to design one for you. If it is the latter, the following points may be useful:

- Set yourself a budget and get several quotes from several cake makers.
- Look in magazines, online or in cake shops for inspiration.
- Ask to taste their cake.
- Ask to see their portfolio of types of cakes they offer.
- Check to see if they can deliver your cake to the venue.

- Ask if the delivery charge is part of the cost of the cake, or if it is extra.

- Book your cake early. Some cake makers, particularly in the high summer season, are booked up months in advance.

> **Tip**
>
> Add strawberries, blueberries, raspberries and softly-whipped cream or ice cream to pieces of cake for dessert. Sponge or chocolate wedding cakes are especially suitable; fruit cakes overwhelm everything.

Alternatives to the wedding cake

The cupcake tower

This innovative practice is gaining in popularity. The tower is a mix of different types of cupcakes which your guests can choose from. Some have orange, lemon or chocolate decorations or icing, with lemon curd, banana, cream cheese additions. Even carrot cake cupcakes can be added to the mix. You can go to town with the icing, adding initials and designs, sprigs of flowers, strawberries and other fruit.

They can be bought ready-made, or you can ask a baker to make them or bake them yourself. Members of the family or friends can also take part.

Make a tiered effect with the cupcakes and place a small wedding cake on the top, decorated with crystalised petals. Get inspiration from magazines, the baker or cake maker. It adds an intimacy to your wedding as everyone gets their individual cupcake.

Cheese cake

There are people out there who don't like cake. If you want a totally differ-ent wedding cake, the cheese cake (no, it's not cheesecake), is a series of layered cheeses, starting with the largest disk at the bottom which is placed on a cake stand, followed by the next largest and so on. Each layer is separated by carboard disk and lilies or other flowers are added to each layer. It can culminate in a topnotch of pale cream roses, for example.

Several companies make these cakes for you (but don't provide the flowers) or you can make your own. For 100 guests count on a 10kg cake (100g per person). Costs vary according to the quality and type of cheese but a rough calculation is around £2 per person — far cheaper than a traditional cake. You can buy twice the quantities needed and use the rest at a later date — some cheeses, particularly blue, freeze won-derfully. For more details look at the House of Cheese website. (www.houseofcheese.co.uk).

Croquembouche

The French do wedding cakes in style. This one is a high cone of prof-iteroles (baked choux pastry filled with crème patissiere — pastry cream) bound with caramel and decorated with threads of caramel, sug-ared almonds, chocolates, flowers or ribbons. The word comes from *croquet en bouche*, meaning 'crunch in the mouth'.

Specialist bakers can make these for you, and one usually serves around 30—40. As they are delicate, packaging and delivery is of the utmost importance. But it is most definitely achievable. The advantage of the *croquembouche* is that it is the dessert, not an add-on like the tradi-tional wedding cake.

French wedding cake

This round chocolate cake is encased with a light icing and is often beautifully decorated in a lace fashion. Ask a French patisserie for advice on how to track one of these lovely creations. They may oblige and make one for you or recommend a company.

The wedding cake: myths and customs

The cake cutting ceremony is a ritual which takes place at the reception, usually after the main meal but it can take place at the beginning of the reception. The bride and groom cut the cake together which symbolises their future.

Cake, or a similar type of confection, has been part of wedding ceremonies for thousands of years. Romans shared a cake made of wheat flour, salt and water, not the sweet one which symbolises unity at today's weddings. In previous times in Britain, flat, round cakes contained fruit and nuts to denote fertility.

Cakes in previous times were thrown over the bride or crumbled over her head, again to denote fertility.

Old English customs include throwing cake on a plate out of the window when the bride returned home to her parents. She would have a happy future if the plate broke but if it didn't she might endure a less than happy marriage. This robust symbolic tradition was to be found in Yorkshire.

Another old English custom was to place a ring in the wedding cake. The guest who found the ring in their the piece of cake would be ensured happiness for the next year.

The shape of the modern three tiered iced cake is reported to have been modelled on London's Bride's Church, rather aptly. It is said that unmarried guests who place a piece of wedding cake under their pillow before sleeping will increase their prospects of finding a partner and bridesmaids who do likewise will dream of their future husbands.

7 Doing your own catering

Let's go back to the basics. What is catering? It's the business of preparing, presenting and serving good food appropriate to a brief — in this case, your wedding.

Let's also examine the strengths you have to carry out the task ahead of you. Although it may be a one-off catering job for you, you should possess some, if not all, of these assets:

● motivation

● organisation

● self-discipline

● a calm nature

● an ability to prioritise

● good delegating skills

● good communication skills.

This chapter will guide you on how to choose a menu to match your skills and the skills of those cooks joining you. It will also help you with the following:

● working out quantities

● preparing your shopping list

● breaking the cooking down into manageable chunks

● sourcing, ordering and storing your food shopping

● timing of food preparation

● setting out a buffet

● serving a three course meal or finger food

● transporting the food to the venue

● keeping safe: food hygiene, refridgeration, storage and temperature; avoiding food posoning.

Choosing a menu

Simplicity is the best way forward; the simpler the food offered the easier and more pleasant it will be for you, your helpers and your guests. No one expects you to become a first class seasoned chef just because you have opted to do your own catering.

First, think about these questions:

- How many guests will you be catering for?
- What do you like to cook?
- What kitchen space and refrigeration is available?
- Who will be helping you?
- What space do you have at your chosen venue?
- Will you be cooking food for a buffet, a two or three course sit-down lunch or dinner, or preparing finger food?

If you are catering for a large number of people, don't be daunted. A buffet or finger food reception is possibly the best way forward as it means you can prepare the food several days in advance, pack it away in the fridge (make sure it's at the right temperature of 4°C and not overcrowded) and be able to concentrate on other things.

If you have decided to go down the sit-down route I suspect that your guest list may be under 40 as it is quite a daunting task – even with the best will in the world – to be calm and measured on the day.

Hog roasts

If you wish to do a simple, yet always pleasing meal, order in a hog roast. Companies who specialise in these will supply the hog, the equipment, staff and other items. Look up hog roasts in your local phone book and get a quote. The companies usually offer to provide salads and other dishes but, if you're looking for quality (most of the salads offered are dull coleslaw or potato salad bought from the cash and carry), just order the hog roast and make your own side dishes such as salads, potato, rice and pasta dishes (some of which are outlined in this chapter).

Buffet menus

Below are some suggestions. Vegetarians are well-catered for; many guests will assume you will be catering for them unless you have can-vassed your guest list and asked each one if they are vegetarian or not. Most meat eaters enjoy vegetarian food too. I suggest making good quan-tities as it is hard to police when guests help themselves to the buffet.

I would also suggest avoiding dishes with avocado (it goes brown quickly even if you've sprinkled it with lemon juice, and can spoil the look of any dish), lamb or pork unless you serve it hot (it can be quite tough cold unless cooked with care), shellfish (unless you know your guests' tastes), dishes that look the same (all beige or white, for exam-ple) or too many dairy or pastry dishes. Balance, colour, simplicity and ease of preparation and serving are what you need to focus on.

Dishes with stars by them have recipes which are found at the end of this chapter.

Menu one

This is one menu which I often cook for weddings and other large par-ties. It looks colourful, has a good variety of dishes to offer your guests of which many are suitable for vegetarians.

- Roasted red and yellow peppers with a mint couscous (V). Can be prepared two days in advance.

- Cold sliced chicken breast with a pine nut, wild rice, lime and mango salad. Can be prepared 36 hours beforehand.

- *Salmon in puff pastry with watercress. Can be prepared 24 hours ahead.

- *Crunchy marinated vegetables (V). Can be prepared 24 hours ahead.

- Green salad with a vinaigrette (V). The vinaigrette can be prepared a week beforehand, the salad arranged in bags and refrigerated the day before.

- Hot new baby potatoes with seasalt (V). This is the only hot dish on the menu and always welcome. The potatoes can be cooked just before you need to serve them and tossed in butter and seasalt with a sprinkling of chives or flat parsley.

- Quality breads and butter.

- One large brie and one other large cheese (V).

- Eton Mess (V). A mixture of meringues, whipped cream, pureed soft fruit and strawberries. The meringues can be made a week in advance, the cream whipped, the fruit pureed 48 hours in advance and refrigerated. The pudding is then assembled just prior to being served.

As you can see, this menu is a very simple one. It has colour and few carbohydrates making it light and extremely tasty. Three of the dishes barely need preparation: the potatoes, the cheeses and the salad.

Menu two

- Smoked haddock mousse. Can be made 36 hours in advance.

- Marinated chicken in a lemon and herb dressing. Can be made 24 hours in advance.

- Pasta, red pepper and baby tomato salad with a pesto sauce (V). Can be made 48 hours in advance.

- Roasted fillet of beef with a horseradish sauce. Can be made 24 hours in advance.

- Crunchy marinated vegetables, green salad, potatoes, breads, cheeses and Eton Mess from the previous menu.

Below are some other suggestions for cold buffet courses which are suitable all year round. Remember that all prepared food should be refrigerated.

Main courses

- Pasta, spinach and Parmesan shaving salad

- Duck breast marinated in soya sauce, garlic and ginger and grilled, served with a puy lentil, onion, ginger and carrot salad with olive oil and lemon dressing

- Spicy tiger prawns in a tomato and herb sauce served with a rice salad

- Carrot, orange and flat parsley salad

- Moroccan chick pea salad

- Coronation chicken with cucumber salad

- Chicken with a tarragon sauce

- Lemon chicken with cold ratatouille

- Peppered beef fillet with a mustard mayonnaise

- Smoked fish shards with spiced rice

- Wild rice, pea, baby leek and saffron pilaff

- Bulgar wheat salad with nuts and apricots

- Mixed leaves and/or baby spinach with bacon bits, walnuts and stilton

- New potato and herb salad mixed with mayo and Greek yoghurt

- Ravioli salad with a pesto dressing.

Desserts

These can precede the cake, or non-traditionalists can have them instead.

- American cheesecake with kiwi fruit and pineapple slices

- Champagne jelly with tuile biscuits

- Pannacotta with poached red fruit

- Chocolate terrine with a red berry sauce

- Exotic fruits in a spicy syrup with mascarpone

- Baked peaches with a macaroon stuffing and raspberry sauce

- Brown sugar meringues with berries and whipped sugared cream

- Glazed cupcakes with homemade chocolate ice cream or caramel ice cream

- Chocolate roulade filled with strawberries and whipped sugared cream, dusted with cocoa powder.

Finger food

Finger food requires no plates as the food is handed around on trays with napkins. I like to serve colourful food which incorporates meat, fish, vegetables and sweet items. I also avoid fiddly finger food which requires a lot of handling, the objective is to be able to prepare simple food, and serve it simply, without too much work.

You can either do only cold food, or a mix of hot and cold if you have help behind the scenes. If you do cold food it can all be prepared in advance and then assembled in the kitchen just before serving. Some of the suggestions below are able to be plated and covered with cling film in advance.

When you are calculating how much to prepare, the rule of thumb is ten bites per person if the food is served over a two hour period, 12–14 if over a longer period of time. If you choose to serve any of the finger food below as canapés with drinks prior to your three course meal or buffet, prepare four per person.

Remember that dishes with stars have recipes at the end of this chapter.

A selection of hot and cold bite-sized food

Cold

- Chicken liver pate in a light pastry case (These cases can be bought – details to follow.) The pate can be made 48 hours in advance.

- Creamy scrambled egg with smoked salmon on rye rounds. Make 24 hours beforehand and assemble prior to serving.

- Smoked salmon on blinis with sour cream and lemon. (Blinis or Russian pancakes can be bought — details to follow.) The salmon can be cut to size, the blinis smeared with dill butter in advance then assembled prior to serving.

- Seared salmon cubes with ginger sauce. These little squares are grilled and can be either hot or cold. Can be made 24 hours in advance and refrigerated.

- Tandoori chicken on a cocktail stick and served with a chilli sauce. These can be grilled 24 hours beforehand and refrigerated. Serve with a small ramekin dish of chilli sauce.

- Satay chicken skewers with a peanut sauce. As above but with a peanut sauce.

- Thai chicken and peanut cakes with a sweet chilli sauce. These cakes can be made 36 hours in advance and refrigerated. Serve with chilli sauce.

- *Asparagus frittata (V). These can be made 24 hours in advance then cut either into wedges or squares.

- Mushroom frittatas (V). As above.

- *Mini Arnold Bennett omelettes. These smoked haddock, cream and egg omelettes can be prepared 24 hours in advance, chilled, then sliced and served.

- Bacon and scallop rolls. These are simplicity itself. Just make sure you use the freshest seafood possible. They can be cooked 24 hours in advance and refrigerated.

- *Thai fishcakes with a soya and ginger or sweet chilli dipping sauce. The fishcakes can be made 36 hours in advance, fried and refrigerated. The sauce can be made several days in advance.

Hot

- *Chipolata sausages with a mustard and honey glaze. These can be cooked 24 hours in advance, refrigerated and re-heated in a honey and mustard sauce.

- Caramelised onion and bacon mini quiches. These can be baked 36 hours ahead of time and re-heated or served cold.

- Ratatouille mini tarts (V). Prepare the ratatouille mix and fill the bought mini cases before serving. Make the ratatouille 48 hours beforehand. For extra bite add a sliver of goat's cheese.

- Thai fishcakes with a soya or chilli dipping sauce. Make these 36 hours in advance, refrigerate and re-heat just before serving.

- Beef and pork mini meatballs with Moroccan spices, served with yoghurt and cucumber. Prepare these 36 hours beforehand, refrigerate and re-heat thoroughly before serving with a yoghurt dip.

- Mini pizzas with mozzarella and olive paste (V). Cut out small pizzas from large ones using a cutter, top with mozzarella and olive paste with a slice of baby tomato, bake, refrigerate and re-heat on the day.

Other hot and cold finger food to consider

- Sushi

- Peking duck rolls

- Bruschetta with a variety of toppings including smoked salmon, capers and sour cream

- Baby potatoes with mock caviar and cream cheese

- Chargrilled vegetable skewers

- Mini hamburgers

- Mini fish and chips

- Mini brownies

- Mini pavlovas (tiny flat meringues topped with small diced fruit and a dab of whipped cream)

- Mini chocolate éclairs (cut good bought ones in half or thirds).

Tip

If you want sushi, find a good supplier who will prepare a fine selection for you and possibly deliver them the day before on disposable trays. Do make sure they are refrigerated until served.

You can buy small pastry cases to fill with ratatouille, chicken liver mousse and other fillings. These can be found in the biscuit section of more upmarket supermarkets and delis. Look out for the name Rahms, a Swedish product I use all the time as the cases are light, un-stodgy and a perfect bite-size. Other makes are heavy and take over, not allowing the filling to speak for itself.

Two or three course sit-down meal menus

It is perfectly possible to cater for a larger wedding by offering a two or three course meal, but it is a daunting prospect for those who are not used to cooking for large numbers. I would limit this type of catering to a small wedding party of perhaps up to 40, but no more, as it can tax even the calmest amongst us. As it is more formal, you also have the added expense of more staff to serve your guests. But, if you have your heart set on a sit-down several course meal, keep it straightforward. What's the mantra? Simple, simple, simple.

Simple is best

Here are some menu suggestions which are made up of dishes that can all be pre-prepared; no twiddly, fiddly last-minute cooking is necessary apart, perhaps, from a vegetable or two. My advice is to ditch the veg – too fiddly and there is a serious chance of over-cooking – and go for potatoes and salad. You can use vegetables in the salads too – far better than offering guests over-cooked, grey, soggy beans and the like. Why make life difficult for yourself when it is totally unnecessary? Simple really is best.

Menu one: two courses with wedding cake as dessert

- *Chicken liver parfait with a fig and onion marmalade served with toasted brioche
- *Salmon in puff pastry with a beurre blanc or hollandaise sauce
- New potatoes with seasalt, butter and flat parsley or chives
- *Bean and shallot salad with vinaigrette
- Assorted breads and cheeses
- Wedding cake with berries, whipped cream or ice cream

All of these dishes can be prepared in advance. The salmon needs to be finished off in the oven, the sauce gently heated (or served cold), the new potatoes cooked and dressed. Plate the fish and place the vegetables in bowls to pass around. Place large cheeses on trays (one for each table) with breads and pass them around. Cut the cake, add the berries and pass the cream or ice cream around.

Menu two: three courses with wedding cake to follow dessert

- Smoked fish mousse with slivers of smoked haddock with a cucumber salad and toasted rye bread
- Fillet of medium-rare beef served cold with a horseradish sauce
- Pommes Dauphinoise – sliced potatoes with cream and garlic
- Green salad with added grilled baby leeks and herbs with a light vinaigrette
- Assorted breads and cheeses
- Chocolate marquise or terrine with a raspberry sauce
- Wedding cake to follow

The advantage of this menu again is that all dishes are pre-prepared and just need to be plated. The fish mousse can already be in ramekin dishes if you have enough. Otherwise, place a large spoonful attractively on each plate. Add the cucumber salad alongside the mousse with the rye bread. Slice the beef and plate it or pass it around on a platter for guests at each table to help themselves. The potatoes just need to be heated through in a low oven then carefully offered to guests in their cooking dish. Toss the salad in the dressing and pass around. The chocolate marquise is sliced and plated, the raspberry sauce added to the plate.

Menu three: a light informal summer lunch

- Chicken salad torn into strips with asparagus, watercress and a lemon and tarragon dressing
- Pasta salad with roasted red and yellow peppers and herbs
- Tomato, basil and buffalo mozzarella salad
- Assorted breads and butter

- Cheeses

- Brown sugar meringues with whipped cream and raspberries

- Wedding cake to follow

All of the above dishes are prepared in advance too and just need assembling prior to serving. You can plate the chicken salad to ensure that everyone gets their fair share and serve the pasta and tomato salad in bowls. You could add hot new potatoes to this meal. Either plate each portion of the meringue dish or get guests to help themselves; each table can have an attractive bowl to share.

Menu four: a two course informal winter lunch

Canapés for your guests with drinks followed by:

- Boeuf Bourguignon or Coq au Vin

- Potato and celeriac puree

- Green bean and cauliflower salad with an olive oil and lemon dressing

- Champagne jelly with tuile biscuits or the wedding cake, or chocolate tart with pineapple

---

Tip

You can cut down the cost of a three course meal by offering your guests a selection of canapés from the above list with drinks, then hand around bowls of the beef or chicken and the puree and salad.

All these dishes can be made in advance and re-heated. Just make sure they are piping hot. The green bean and cauliflower salad (blanched and refreshed beans and cauliflower florets) can be dressed just prior to serving. For a triumphal end, serve the jelly in tall champagne flutes — when preparing the jelly, put the mixture in flutes to set. Just make sure you have sufficient fridge space to fit them in. By offering a jelly after a meaty main course you keep heaviness at bay.

Food quantities

This often perplexes people when they are catering for large numbers, and the result more often than not is that a lot of food is thrown out thanks to over-ordering. Obviously the last thing the hosts wants is for guests to go hungry. This is after all, a celebration and food and drink are very much part of the ritual. Getting it spot on is, of course, nigh on impossible — some guests are exceptionally fond of their food — but the following guidance will help.

When calculating how much food you need for your buffet, look at the most popular dishes and double the amount as you don't want to run out of those particular ones.

Meat, chicken, beef, lamb, pork, duck, veal, venison and other game

- 225g per person from a roast
- 140g per person for stews and casseroles (if the dish has other main ingredients such as mushrooms and shallots), otherwise increase the meat content to 225g
- 125g for buffets if other dishes such as fish are also offered
- ribs: three per person
- One chicken breast per person if a main course dish, otherwise $\frac{1}{2}$ a breast if part of a buffet consisting of other meat and fish

- quail: one per person if part of a buffet, otherwise two if offered as a main course

- grouse, partridge or pigeon: one per person

Fish and seafood

- 220g filleted fish per person for a main course

- 85–115g per person for a buffet if serving meat or poultry as well

- lobster: one small one per person for a main course or half if large; half for a first course

- scallops: four large ones for a main course, two large ones, sliced, for a first course;

- fish pate or mousse: around 150g per person — more if less rich fish is used

Vegetables and salads

- prepared vegetables: 115g per person if served with another vegetable

- salad leaves (washed and picked over): 60g per person for a first course or buffet or 30g for a main course

- potatoes: 180g per person (unpeeled weight) new potatoes: 115g per person, or five to six per person of small, new ones

Rice, pasta, grains, pulses (puy lentils and chick peas, for example)

- rice: 30g per person with a main course or in a salad

- pasta and noodles: 85g per person for a first course, 140g for a main course or 30g with a main course and two vegetables or buffet

- lentils, chick peas, beans, couscous: 60g per person with a main course or as part of a buffet salad

Dairy produce

- cheese: 115g per person, or half if part of a buffet

- butter: 30g per person with bread or biscuits with cheese

- cream or milk with tea or coffee: 85 ml per person

- ice cream: 140ml on its own or 50 ml if served with a dessert

Other ingredients

- small rolls: two per person

- large rolls: one per person

- mousses, parfaits, terrines: 120–150g per person depending on the content (with strong fish or chocolate, less is needed)

- fresh fruit salad: 115g per person

- sweet or savoury tarts: a 30 cm tart gives eight to ten portions depending on the type

- sauces to go with meat or fish: 30 ml per person

- mayonnaise: 30 ml per person

- vinaigrette: 30 ml per person

> **Tip**
>
> When making couscous, lentils, pasta, carrot salad or potato salad, measure out a portion into another container using a heaped serving spoon, counting the portions and marking them down. This way you can be sure of having enough. This method can be used to measure any type of dish such as fruit salad or sauce. You be the judge of what the most popular dishes are – and remember to double up on the spoon count.

Canapés

Choose food that will give a variety of texture, flavour and colour. You may wish to offer your guests a mix of savoury and sweet. At a wedding reception, for example, 12 savoury (a mix of vegetarian and meat or fish) and three sweet canapés.

- pre-meal canapés with drinks: four per person

- a wedding party lasting two hours: ten per person

- a wedding reception without a meal afterwards: 12–14 per person

Serving the food

Tips for serving canapés

- Have different types of serving dishes. Some canapés look terrific on glass, others on white china or multi-coloured dishes.

- Make canapés bite-sized.

- Avoid over-garnishing: it isn't practical and looks messy; delicate herbs and salad leaves soon wilt.

- Start with cold canapés and offer hot ones after the majority of guests have arrived.

- Offer small napkins.

- If using cocktail sticks make sure those handing out the food take away the used ones or they may be used twice.

- You can never have enough chipolata sausages glazed with honey and Dijon mustard.

Tips for buffet service

- Have several 'stations' (several tables put together for food service) if the guest list is significant. This way, guests can be served the same dishes from different stations which avoids a mad scramble.

- Place plates, cutlery and napkins at both ends of the buffet tables to lessen the queue, and let the guests know.

- Communicate with guests where they need to go. They may just join a queue and not be aware there is another station to go to.

- Make sure you have a lot of serving spoons. They get moved from dish to dish unless guests are served by staff behind the buffet stations.

- Invite tables to the buffet table one by one, rather than having a lengthy queuing free-for-all.

- Replenish dishes quickly and tidily or have dishes in the kitchen ready to come out to replace empty ones.

- Tidy up the buffet as service proceeds. There is nothing worse than guests who haven't been to the buffet seeing a food bomb-site.

- Make sure all guests have visited the buffet before offering seconds.

- If possible, place desserts plus plates, bowls and cutlery at separate stations.

- If space permits, have coffee and tea at separate stations or clear the main buffet before laying out the hot drink service.

- Make sure that there is good space between buffet tables and guests' tables so that a bottleneck doesn't start. Having to put up with queues of people by your left ear or right hand can make guests feel uncomfortable.

> ## Tip
>
> For a sense of drama use this catering company trick: napkin-covered pedestals or boxes add different levels to your table for highlighting a dessert, the cheeseboard or a sumptuous bread display. Use the pedestals to create, depth, variety and a feeling of the land of plenty.

Tips for serving a two or three course meal

- Make sure you have enough space in the kitchen where you and your helpers will be working to plate up. If you can only plate up five first courses at a time it may be a long wait for some guests.

- Count the plates for each course. You don't want to be short of a plate or two and not be able to serve some guests. The same goes for glasses and cutlery.

- Have a clearing-up area up and running. When plates come back into the kitchen your helpers don't want them to be put in just any old place as it will interfere with the next course. Have a bin ready for leftovers, and boxes ready for empty bottles.

- Be sure to delegate and inform your staff or friends and family (if they are helping you) what you wish them to do. Write a list of jobs and give it to each helper so they know what duties to carry out — and when. Just remember that some may not be used to this kind of work so be patient. Brief them beforehand.

How to shop

This may sound as if I'm teaching the proverbial granny to suck eggs but it is crucial to know when to shop and how to store your food purchases. It is also vital to know when to order specialist produce so that your chosen dishes can feature on the menu you have been working on.

First of all, have you chosen your menu? Congratulations on this mean feat! You've taken into consideration your guests' needs (vegetarians, allergies, perhaps cultural or religious diets) and you're raring to go.

If you have free-range or organic chicken on the menu have you found a good supplier? The same goes for other produce such a beef fillet (shop around), venison, quail or other game. If you have decided on salmon, which type will you buy (wild, organic or farmed?). Get several quotes from different suppliers, including supermarkets, and once you have decided which supplier you would like to use, order in advance. Specify if you would like each fish fillet cut into a specific size, for example, how you would like them packaged and when you would like them delivered or when to pick the supplies up.

Refrigeration

- Do you have enough refrigeration?
- Is your fridge/fridges set at the right temperature? 4°C is the right temperature.
- Will you hire a commercial-type fridge if your party is a large one?
- Can you set aside a clean, dry area for all dry goods and other produce?

Before doing any ordering, taste, taste, taste. Bargain. Ask for wholesale prices if you're buying in bulk. Go to farmers' markets, farm shops and other outlets for local produce. See it as a delicious, exciting challenge rather than a tiresome chore.

Your shopping list

Make a list of all the ingredients. Put them under headings such as meat, fish, vegetables, dairy, dry stores (tins, rice, pasta, salt, pepper, olive oil, chocolate, coffee, sugar, etc), decorations (flowers and other items) and miscellaneous purchases (paper napkins, washing up liquid, paper towels, etc). Next to these items put where you will be buying them from and when you need to buy them. You could use colour coding to focus your attention on each type of purchase.

Timeline

1   Order your main ingredients and specify a date for delivery or collection. For meat, fish and other perishables, depending on their shelf life, it should be around three to five days before starting to cook.

2   Once you have finalised your dry goods list, shop around to see where the best deals can be found. Always bear in mind quality over quantity. Don't be tempted to impulse-buy as you could end up with ingredients you will not use, creating a hole in your budget. It may also mean that if you do buy items not on the list, you create an imbalance on your menu. Stick to the plan.

3   Order all dairy and perishable goods a good three weeks to a month beforehand. Arrange the time of collection or delivery. Make sure you have allocated space in the fridge or kitchen or other suitable area to store them properly.

4   Check all your ordered goods either when you collect them or on delivery. If you don't you may be missing vital items or the quality may not up to scratch. If so, contact your suppliers and tell them immediately so that the situation can be rectified.

5   Cross each item off when it is bought.

6 Keep a running total of purchases and check it against your budget.

7 Keep all receipts just in case you need to return or exchange any goods bought.

8 There is no need to take up valuable space your house or garage with wine, beers, water and other drinks. Ask your supplier to store them for you once you have paid for them. They often deliver too. Unfortunately supermarkets and some wine merchants don't offer this service so if you have limited space ask before buying. Secure any alcohol in a safe place, not a garage from where it may be stolen.

Tip

Carry a notebook with your list written down and do spot checks on prices.

Timeplan for cooking

As previously mentioned, don't be tempted to cook for the freezer. Choose a simple, fresh, practical yet sparklingly delicious menu which you can prepare as close to the wedding as possible. Frozen, microwaved food is a no-no in my book; the taste is nothing close to spanking fresh food.

Start by making a list of the following:

- dishes to be prepared the week before (items such as ice creams for the freezer and meringues, for example, which have a good shelf life)

- dishes to be prepared four days before

- three days before

- two days before

- the day before

- on the day.

Transporting your food

When you transport food from one premises to another — from the supermarket and farmers' market to home or the venue where the wedding reception will take place — it is vital to keep it from becoming contaminated with dirt or bacteria. Animals' baskets, hairs, muddy boots and other potential hazards should be removed from your vehicle and the car or van kept in a clean condition.

- Food should be transported in suitable packaging or containers to prevent contamination. For example, don't use used plastic bags or open containers.

- The containers mustn't have been used for other purposes. Emptying out a nail box and adding food to it is perhaps an extreme example, but you get the drift.

- Raw and cooked foods need to be kept separate.

- All food must be labelled. Those involved with the food preparation will panic if they can't find a container as nothing has been labelled, and valuable time is taken up by looking into each container until the right one is found.

- Label your boxes: put the date the food was made and by whom. Also, add in a different colour what needs to be refrigerated and what needs to be kept in a cool, dry place.

> ## Tip
>
> Make sure you have sharp knives before starting the marathon cook-in. This way you will save yourself potential injury. Blunt knives cause accidents, not the other way around. Buy some good ones — they will last you a lifetime.

Hygiene standards

Spillages and other accidents

- Always clean up any spillages immediately to prevent slipping.

- Broken glass needs to be wrapped in newspaper before it goes into a bin.

- Avoid putting debris from ashtrays into bins as cigarette butts could still be going and could light up paper.

- Have a first aid box handy with some plasters and burns ointment. Take it with you to the wedding venue.

Avoiding food poisoning

Although you and those preparing the food may not be professional caterers, you have to make sure that the food is stored, cooked and served in a responsible manner in order to avoid food poisoning. Here are some vital tips:

- Always ensure that those who are preparing food wash their hands when entering the kitchen and that after a cigarette or toilet break they wash them again properly.

- Cover food left to cool to avoid contamination (from flies, coughs and sneezes, for example).

133

- Don't take chances with food that has been unrefrigerated for a long time after a function. Throw it out, especially if the food has been in a warm environment.

- Don't put food which is still warm in the fridge — wait until it is cooled. By adding warm or hot food to the fridge, the temperature will rise and bacteria will grow.

- Cover food in the fridge with a lid, foil or cling film to avoid drying out and cross-contamination.

- Always store raw and cooked food on different shelves. Raw meat should go on the bottom shelf.

- Don't wrap cheese or meats in cling film — use greaseproof paper or place in a container with a lid. This way they won't sweat and will keep fresh for longer.

- When storing salad leaves and herbs add a layer of kitchen paper to soak up excess moisture.

- Always tidy up your kitchen space, wash your surfaces thoroughly and do the washing up before starting on another dish. This way you will minimise any risk of cross-contamination and it will help the smooth running of the kitchen.

- Make a point of labelling anything that goes in your fridge with contents, date and portion amount.

- Keep your paperwork out of the kitchen if possible as they pick up moisture and grease and can add bacteria.

- Don't prepare a sandwich on a board which has just been used to cut up raw poultry or other meat, as it can lead to cross-contamination.

Tip

Change dishcloths frequently! Old, soiled ones have loads of bacteria. Don't use one to mop up the floor then clean the countertop space. (As if!)

Most common bugs

There are six types of bugs which can happen to those who don't follow commonsensical ways with food as listed above. I'll just point out three of them. If you are concerned and wish to know more, contact your local district council's environmental health office.

Campylobactor: this is the most common. It is found in raw and under-cooked poultry, red meat, unpasteurised milk and untreated water.

Salmonella: the second most common bug is found in eggs, raw meat, poultry, unpasteurised milk, yeast and even in coconut and chocolate. It passes easily from person to person through poor hygiene such as not washing hands, or picking noses.

Clostridium perfringens: this third most common bug is found in soil, sewage, animal manure and in the gut of humans and animals. It breeds in food cooked slowly in large quantities then left to stand for a long time.

Tip

Leaving raw or cooked chicken out in a hot kitchen without covering it for several hours is asking for trouble. Even when covered, it shouldn't be there but in a fridge.

Recipes

Below are seven recipes, mentioned earlier, which you may wish to try. Follow the notes on each one to adapt the quantities.

Crunchy vegetables

For eight. Double or treble the recipe for 16 or 24 – and so on – guests.

Now that our tastebuds prefer more crunchy vegetables to boiled-to-extinction ones, this recipe is the perfect dish for parties. It fulfils the need to add vegetables to the mix but doesn't require any last-minute cooking. I hope you will find it a real godsend of a dish. Keep an eye on the vegetables when steaming them as they can cook faster than you think. You can add cherry tomatoes and olives too for extra taste, or sprinkle some feta cubes over the salad to make a complete dish.

2 heads of cauliflower, cut into florets

400g French beans, topped and tailed if wished

400g baby carrots, topped and tailed if wished

400g baby leeks, cleaned and left whole

4 tbsp flat parsley, chopped

2 tbsp mint, chopped

For the marinade

350ml extra virgin olive oil

juice and grated rind of three lemons

seasalt and freshly milled black pepper

Steam each vegetable separately until al dente (just cooked: maybe 5–6 minutes only) and plunge into iced water to stop them from cooking further.

Drain thoroughly and pat dry.

Mix the marinade together and heat up in a pan over a low heat.

Put the vegetables in a large bowl, add the warm marinade and gently turn.

Add the herbs and marinate for 24 hours.

Serve with all kinds of meats or fish and bread to mop up the juices.

Salmon in puff pastry:

For 8: If you wish to make this dish for larger quantities simply multiply by the number of people you wish to cook it for. For example, make ten of these for 80 people.

1.5 kg salmon fillets cut into two equal pieces

seasalt and freshly milled pepper

a good handful of tarragon leaves

85g unsalted butter at room temperature

1 x 375g pack of fresh puff pastry (found in good supermarkets)

1 beaten egg

Remove any lingering bones from the fish on a wooden board.

Strip the tarragon leaves from the stems, chop finely then mix with the softened butter.

Add small dots of the flavoured butter on top of one fish fillet, then place the other one on top.

Flour the counter with a handful of flour. Roll out the puff pastry into two strips long enough to accommodate the fish.

Place the fish on one strip of pastry, then add the second strip, brush the bottom strip with beaten egg to act as a seal and pinch both pastry strips together to seal the fish.

Refrigerate until ready to cook. Note: you can prepare up to this point 24 hours beforehand then bake.

Brush the pastry with the remainder of the beaten egg.

Add a pattern to the pastry by making long criss-crosses lightly on the surface with a sharp knife.

Place on a baking tin and bake in a pre-heated oven (gas 5, 190°C) for around 50 minutes or until the pastry is cooked and golden.

Test the fish to see if it is cooked by inserting the point of a knife.

Serve it either hot or cold with a beurre blanc or hollandaise sauce.

Chicken liver parfait

This makes between ten and 12 portions. As it is rich, slice accordingly. Serve with a chutney made of figs and onion, or other fruit and veg-etable combinations and with toasted brioche. You can re-make the recipe for larger numbers: three times the recipe (make individually) is enough for 30 or more people. It can be made a good 48 hours ahead of time and chilled. The chutney can be made well in advance — two to three weeks — and chilled.

800g chicken livers

85g onions, diced

1 or 2 garlic cloves, diced

250g unsalted butter

1 egg, beaten

handful of thyme, leaves removed and chopped

3 tbsp port, Madeira or good brandy

seasalt and freshly milled pepper

Prepare a terrine tin or long bread tin by lining it with greaseproof paper, or use a non-stick loaf tin. Stand this in a roasting tin and pour in water to come halfway up the sides of the terrine or loaf tin.

Heat the oven to gas 2/150°C.

Sweat the onion and garlic in 30g of the butter.

Reduce the chosen alcohol in a small pan with the thyme leaves.

Liquidise the trimmed chicken livers, and add the onion, garlic and the alcohol, then gradually add the remaining butter which has been melted over a low heat.

Season with salt and pepper. Test the liver mix by cooking a teaspoon of it in butter. Add more seasoning if necessary.

Pour the mix into the container and bake for 25 minutes or until set.

Dip a knife point into the terrine to see if it is cooked. If it comes out clean, it is.

Cool and refrigerate. To serve, turn the container upside down, remove the paper and slice into ten or 12 even slices.

Asparagus and spinach frittata

For four as a starter or cut up into squares for a canapé which will give around ten per frittata. As this is made in an omelette pan (with a handle which can go in the oven) you will need to make each one individually.

225g asparagus cut into small pieces, around one inch long

2 shallots, finely diced

20g butter

2 handfuls of fresh baby spinach

5 large eggs, beaten with 2 tbsp milk or single cream

2 tbps freshly grated Parmesan

freshly milled black pepper

Pre-heat the oven to gas 6 200°C.

Poach the asparagus in water and drain when just cooked through but not soggy.

Sauté the shallots in the butter in an omelette pan until softened.

Beat the eggs, adding some black pepper.

Add half the eggs to the pan, place the spinach and asparagus evenly on the eggs, add the parmesan then cover with the remaining egg.

Make sure the vegetables are covered with the egg mix. If not, beat another egg with some cream and pour over.

Bake the frittata for around eight minutes or until the egg is set.

Cool and refrigerate. Cut into wedges or squares just before serving. Can be served hot or cold.

Omelette Arnold Bennett

This recipe makes 20 rounds of delectable haddock and cheese omelette. Cut just before serving so the slices don't dry out. Make the same recipe again for another 20, and so on. Add other fish such as smoked salmon if you wish, in which case there is no need to cook it.

3 eggs, separated

1 tbsp double cream

2 tbsp freshly grated Parmesan cheese

freshly milled black pepper

120g cooked, flaked smoked haddock or other smoked fish

2 tbsp whipped cream

2 cherry tomatoes, chopped

1 tbsp chopped chives

Pre-heat the oven to gas 5/190°C.

Line a Swiss roll tin with greaseproof paper.

Mix the egg yolks with the double cream and cheese.

Whisk the egg whites until stiff.

Fold into the yolks. Season with black pepper.

Spread the mix over the greaseproof paper, filling the surface, and bake for 10–12 minutes. Cool.

Mix the haddock with the whipped cream, tomatoes and chives. Season to taste.

Peel the omelette off the lining paper, place it on a board and spread with the haddock mix.

Roll up into a cylinder like a swiss roll and cut into rolls just before serving.

Thai fishcakes

This recipe makes 24. Use fish that hasn't been frozen as too much moisture can be added to the mixture. You don't need expensive cod or haddock – go for cheaper types of white fish. Double for 48, treble for 72 and so on.

500g firm white fish such as hake, cut into chunks

2 tsp red chillies, chopped

2 tbsp coriander, chopped

4 kaffir lime leaves, finely shredded

2 lemongrass, outer layer removed and finely chopped

2 shallots, peeled and finely diced

2 garlic cloves, peeled and finely chopped

1 tbsp fish sauce (nam pla)

1 tsp soya sauce

2 tsp palm or brown sugar

vegetable oil for frying

sweet chilli sauce for dipping

Place the fish in a food processor and process until relatively smooth.

Add all the other ingredients except for the vegetable oil and chilli sauce and process until combined, around 10–20 seconds. Do not over-process.

Remove from the processor and form into 24 patties or balls.

Refrigerate.

Heat the oil until hot and cook them in batches. Drain on kitchen paper.

Eat immediately or cook and refrigerate, serving either cold or hot with the chilli sauce.

Chipolata sausages with a honey and mustard glaze

This canapé is the most moreish of the lot. Choose an excellent chipolata sausage. One pack of ten makes 20. Do the maths for more. You can make these in advance (two or three days) and refrigerate. Re-heat them thoroughly before serving, or serve cold.

1 pack of ten chipolata sausages, each sausage twisted in half and cut with a knife

5 tbsp Dijon mustard

5 tbsp runny honey

Pre-heat the oven to gas 7/220°C.

Place the chipolata sausages, now halved, into a greased ovenproof dish and bake until cooked through. They should take around 20–25 minutes.

Drain the sausages from the fat.

Mix the mustard and honey together.

Pour over the hot sausages and coat.

Serve immediately or cool and refrigerate. They can be re-heated. Serve with a cocktail stick.

Bean and shallot salad

Cook french beans until just done.

Rinse under a cold tap until cool.

Drain and pat dry.

Add shallots sautéd in butter and cooled.

Dress with olive oil, lemon, black pepper and seasalt.

Add a little Dijon mustard for an extra kick.

8 Planning the drinks

You have decided on the food menu; now it's time to think about the drink. If you haven't given a large party before you might be unsure about the amount and type of drinks you will need.

You may be catering for different age groups and social backgrounds. Drinks are an important part of the equation; it is crucial to get it right, and to avoid the British propensity to binge drink (something I am sure you would like to avoid happening at your wedding).

This chapter will cover:

- the pros and cons of a cash bar

- types of drinks to offer – and avoid

- how to set up and manage your bar

- your drinks budget

- amounts to buy

- sale or return

- hiring glasses and other equipment for the bar

- managing staff or volunteer family and friends

- how to manage toasts

- alcohol concerns: the curse of the binge drinker and under-age drinkers.

Your drinks budget

The average bride and groom will spend approximately 40% of their budget on food, the cake and alcohol. You should budget for approximately half a bottle of wine per person for lunch, $\frac{3}{4}$ bottle in the evening, one or two pre-reception drinks (it depends how quickly you move your guests on to the food) and a glass of champagne or sparkling wine to toast the bridal pair. Also factor in water and soft drinks.

The traditional wedding vs the cash bar

What would you like to offer your guests to drink? You could go the traditional way and offer champagne on arrival at the reception along with, perhaps, a choice of red or white wine, orange juice and water. Followed by a choice of red and white wine with the meal or reception? Finishing with a champagne toast.

Or, if you have limited funds to spend on alcohol, you could have a cash bar. You might prefer to do this, but when guests arrive at the reception offer them a first drink and champagne for toasting the bridal pair.

Points for and against a cash bar:

- It can be seen as tacky and lacking in generosity.
- It can limit the amount of alcohol your guests will buy, therefore limiting drunken behaviour.

I personally feel that you should stick to your budget and only invite the number of guests you can afford to enjoy your day. This way you celebrate with your nearest and dearest and give all a good time at your wedding. Some weddings go down the cash bar route to save money but I would suggest that, from a hospitable point of view you add a drink to your budget so that your guests are made to feel welcome.

What to offer

When you set out your budget, you included wine and possibly champagne or sparkling wine. Beer too, I bet, and water and soft drinks. In America, the hard stuff is considered normal, and cocktails, bourbon, gin, brandy, rum and other spirits are on offer at weddings. Although there are more cocktails to be found in the average British bar or pub in recent years, it hasn't caught on here to any extent; wine and beer are the usual drinks to be found at a wedding. I would suggest it is not necessary to have a complete bar, either paid or unpaid.

Cash bar options

If you feel a cash bar is for you, here are some tips:

- Offer wine and beer only so that you don't end up with a lot of half-empty bottles of vodka, gin, whisky and brandy. Even if your favourite aunt can't live without her gin she'll make it through the day with other offerings.

- Ensure that soft drinks are served too. If your guests go to the bar to buy drinks, they will want to get all types, not just alcohol.

- Make sure you brief your staff on all drinks and don't charge for water or juices. This would be too ungenerous for words.

- Have chilled wines and beer on offer. Your guests will feel doubly unwelcome if you ask them to pay for their drinks and take no care in how they are served.

- Have good glasses: Paris goblets don't allow for the wine to breathe and develop properly. A glass with tapering sides and a larger bowl make any wine better.

- Offer ice and lemon and make the bar look attractive.

- Have a lot of change so that those in charge of the bar aren't going through their own pockets trying to find the right change. Keep the money in a proper cash box for security reasons and keep an eye on it.

> **Tip**
>
> Food is the best way to soak up alcohol as it slows the rate of absorption in the body. (Just beware of salty food which will require more drinking to quench the thirst that salt creates.) Water or soft drinks are also crucial in limiting the amount of alcohol in the blood so, like precious flowers, hydrate your guests by offering water on trays with alcoholic drinks before the meal, place bottles of water – and keep replenishing them – on the tables and continue to offer water throughout the party.

Finding your wedding wines

Here are some suggestions which will help you make informed choices.

- Decide on what you would like to serve your wedding guests.

- Shop around: most wine merchants, supermarkets and French-based wine companies have internet lists.

- Many independent wine merchants offer better value, lesser-known wines, and their staff are trained to give advice, unlike supermarkets or cash and carry.

- Taking a van across the Channel to fill up is another well-worn route. The disadvantage is that you can't return unopened cases of drink, unlike independent wine merchants which offer a sale or return basis.

- Independent wine merchants, unlike supermarkets, often have wines to try before you take the plunge to buy.

- There are many excellent wines at around £5 a bottle. There is no need to buy expensive ones. But if someone offers to pay for the wine as a wedding present, your budget may receive a boost.

- Marry your wine with your food: full-bodied whites and reds are excellent for autumn and winter, citrussy whites, rosés and light-bodied reds perfect for spring and summer weddings.

- If you are using caterers, they may be able to suggest suitable wines to go with the food.

Champagne and sparkling wine

Most people getting married think of drinking champagne at their wedding and guests think along the same lines as it is seen as the drink of celebration. Will you choose bottles, magnums, white, pink, vintage, non-vintage champagne, or go for the cheaper option — sparkling wine?

How are they made?

They are wines containing bubbles of carbon dioxide, bottled under pressure. There are three methods of production: the *méthode champenoise* in which the wine undergoes a second fermentation in the bottle, the tank or bulk method, in which the wine is bottled while still fermenting slightly, and thirdly, the addition of carbon dioxide gas while bottling.

Wine produced outside the Champagne region of France may not be called champagne, even if this method is used.

Lightly sparkling wines are known as *pétillante* or *frizzante*; they are often young wines which are bottled while still fermenting, such as lambrusco and the Portuguese vinho verde.

Champagne and sparkling wine suggestions

There are so many choices in today's marketplace; here are some suggestions to make it easier for you to come to a conclusion.

- Go for lesser-known labels to keep the costs down. This applies to both champagne and sparkling wine.

- A non-vintage wine has a smooth, rounded style that is good for a toast or when offering a glass to guests on arrival.

- For a hot summer's day reception choose a lighter, elegant Billecart-Salmon or Nicolas Feuillatte to go with your canapés.

- A more full-bodied one for autumn and winter might be Bollinger, Pol Roger or Jacquart.

- A pink fizz for the toast may be a good choice, such as Billecart-Salmon Rosé or Laurent-Perrier.

- If going down the sparkling wine route consider top new world wines like Deutz, Green Point, Cuvée Napa and Jansz. Sussex Nyetimber is a truly remarkable British award-winning sparkling wine that equals a good champagne.

- You can always cut costs by making buck's fizz from a good sparkling wine and proper orange juice (not the concentrated stuff which bears little resemblance to the orange).

- Or you can add cassis to your champagne or sparkling wine — or offer a selection of unadulterated wine, buck's fizz or cassis.

- Serve your champagne or sparkling wine either in fashionable bowl-shaped glasses or, if you wish to preserve those bubbles longer, go for a flute.

- If your caterer is supplying the champagne or sparkling wine — or any of the other wines — ensure that you have a tasting of all choices in order to make an informed decision.

- Buy by the case rather than by the bottle: it works out more cheaply — as anyone who has been into a Majestic warehouse will know.

General wine tips

- High-quality sparkling wines come from the cooler regions of Australia, New Zealand, California and Britain thanks to their chalky soils and long growing season.

- The cooler the climate, the leaner the alcohol content. German wines, for example, range from 10–12% in many cases.

- Conversely, hotter climates produce more robust wines and the alcohol content can reaching preposterously high percentages – 15% is almost the norm.

- Check when buying your wine that the alcohol content is a more manageable 12–13% as your guests may not realise its potency and drink more than they normally do – with adverse results.

- Traditionally, white wine went with fish, red with meat. There are no hard and fast rules these days. A light fish, however, won't benefit from a robust red; an oilier fish, might.

- Buy in advance: buy in seasonal sales but choose wisely, not just because something is cheap.

- Don't serve different wines at the top table. It's a real slap in the face for lesser mortals!

- For real pzazz, choose wine in large bottles – it really adds to the atmosphere. But make sure you can chill them properly; if you choose white, rose, champagne or sparkling wine, your fridge space or chilling methods (use a large bin with ice and water) are of paramount importance.

- Avoid well-known name brands. Your guests will know how much you have spent – or not – on your wine choice.

- Lock your own cellar door (or equivalent) for obvious reasons.

Serving wine

Paris goblets, those little squat glasses, have had their day. Go for plain, clear-stemmed glass that can either be hired or lent for nothing from wine merchants or supermarkets. Be sure to order them well in advance (in summer in particular) as there is a finite number. They must be returned clean.

Make sure that glasses are clean and there is no washing up liquid on them, which can ruin the contents. Glasses should be presented bowl up at table, not bowl-down as this can trap stale air.

Chill white wines but not overly so as this can dull their aroma and flavour. When putting wines out to warm, don't put them near radiators, in a hot kitchen or by bright lights or they will taste like soup.

When pouring wine avoid over-filling the glass; it should be half to two thirds full. Instruct your staff or helpers on how to pour wine.

Serving champagne or sparkling wine

Most white wines, champagnes and sparkilng wines, benefit from being quite cold — at least an hour in the fridge. But bear in mind that if a fridge is stuffed to the gunnels with bottles, the temperature doesn't reach the setting at which the fridge is set for a while. Check the temperature in the fridge and set it to a low point before adding bottles. Chill them for a period longer than an hour — as long as possible.

- One way of chilling the bottles is to plunge them into wine buckets or a large plastic bin for larger parties; add ice and water halfway up.

- Dry the bottle if there is a lot of water dripping from it.

- Avoid shaking the bottle before opening it.

- Place the bottle on a flat surface and put a cloth or napkin over it to prevent an unplanned cork escape.

- Keep the cork facing away from you and others around you.

- Keep one hand firmly on the top with the cork; the other hand should unwind the wire cage to remove it.

- Hold the cork down with one hand. Hold the bottle at a 45-degree angle and slowly turn the bottle.

- Never twist the cork.

- The bubbles will slowly start to push the cork up. Keep a firm grip on the cork and slowly allow it to ease out with a gentle sigh.

- Have glasses ready in which to pour the champagne or sparkling wine.

Water, beer and soft drinks

Water is essential to offer your guests. Wedding parties can last for many hours and water helps to keep your guests hydrated and to counteract the amount of alcohol they may drink. Offer still and sparkling water and keep replenishing bottles on tables or on drinks trays. If you want to be a bit smarter, choose glass over plastic.

Beer

Many younger guests like beer, and the choice is staggering. There are full-bodied bitters, pale bitters, malty ales, stouts, porters, Belgian and Bavarian wheat beers, German lagers, strong dark lagers, Trappist ales, smoked beers, strong India Pale Ales (IPA), floral-hopped beers, fruity beers and ginger spiced beers, to say nothing of the vast range of local beers and ales. Real Ale enthusiasts have their own likes and dislikes. Someone close to you will have their preferences and can guide you as to which ones to choose.

Getting in a beer keg

If you might have a lot of beer drinkers coming to your wedding, consider renting a keg. It's rather more festive than drinking from a bottle. Beers, as wines, have become higher in alcohol too so make sure you read the labels before buying. Some guests seeing beer as a quite an innocuous drink rather than realising its alcohol content. If the ABV, (alcohol by volume), of a beer is 5% or over it is considered a strong beer. 3–5% is an average ABV.

Although I haven't used one, there are companies that rent kegs. They offer a service of all types of beers and ciders. Some also offer a mobile bar service which they stock and staff. There are several companies who rent kegs: look on the internet or contact one of your local breweries who may be happy to oblige.

Soft drinks

There is a vast choice of soft drinks which can come in cans, bottles or concentrated. The latter is a cheaper option, but you will need jugs and someone to take care of it. Remember to have ice and lemon to add to the jugs.

Shop around at your local supermarkets for price comparison but don't be tempted to buy a huge stock as you may be drinking a lot of soft drinks for some considerable time in the future. Depending on the length of the wedding, buy two cans per child and extra for those who may not be drinking.

Tea and coffee

Contrary to popular belief, drinking coffee to sober up doesn't work. But do offer your guests a good cup of coffee or tea after your wedding meal. I suggest hiring cafetieres, the best route to good coffee-making. Plan on hiring one per table of 8. (I'll give you a list of equipment to hire in the next chapter.)

Have a selection of teas — breakfast, Earl Grey and peppermint are the most popular — and hire in tea pots too for the occasion.

Managing staff, or volunteer friends and family, with the bar

I'll cover staffing in Chapter 9 but I'll add just a word or two here about their involvement with the drinks.

If asking friends and family, only ask those over 18 to be involved as it is illegal for those under this age to be serving drinks or taking money at a cash bar. You will undoubtedly choose responsible people to help you, not those whose prime function might be to over-indulge. Brief your friends, family or staff on what, how and when you would like drinks to be served and keep up the communication with them during the party.

Go through the drinks list with them, showing them the bottles to be used and when they are to be opened and poured. If you think it is a good idea, make a clear list of when to serve which type of wine, champagne or sparkling wine and the chosen wine for the toast. Ask them to circulate with bottles to top up glasses, tell them when to hold back, when and how to clear glasses (never by fingers in the bowl but holding the stem or base), and where they should put them afterwards.

Glass requirement and bar set up

For every ten adults plan to have:

- 20 glasses for two types of wine, if offering red and white
- 15 glasses for beers, water and soft drinks
- 15 champagne flutes or wine glasses for reception drinks
- 40 glasses for a three hour drinks and finger food reception.

Glass sizes

- If you use small glasses you increase the amount of work for staff, and if self-serve or queuing at the bar, small glasses will create a larger queue.

- Go for 180ml glasses for wine for a 150ml serving.

- Go for 180ml glasses for water, soft drinks or vodka or whisky.

- Choose either a 240ml or 300ml glass for beer.

- If serving cocktails go for the right type of glass such as a V-shaped one for martinis. They look smart and give a sophisticated edge to the party.

Measurements

There are:

- five 150ml glasses of wine or champagne in a 750ml bottle

- six 150ml glasses in a litre and ten in a 1.5 litre bottle.

- 60 measures in a 750ml bottle of whisky, vodka, gin or other spirits, 22 in a litre bottle and 39 in a 1.5 litre bottle.

Bar set up

The following list gives an outline of what a bar might be stocked with:

- glasses for wine, beer, soft drinks and champagne

- ice buckets, bottle opener, corkscrew, ice tongs, napkins

- mixers such as coca cola, soda, tonic, ginger ale, sparkling and still water

- lemon slices, olives (if preparing cocktails), toothpicks.

> ## Tip
>
> If there will be children and/or you are going to be outside where glass may prove hazardous, buy some attractive plastic or disposable glasses to place on your bar.

Wedding toasts

Toasts are very much a part of special occasions in our lives. Weddings are a natural place for such celebratory words: toasting the bride, groom and other members of the bridal party.

At a wedding reception where a meal is served, toasts are usually offered at the end of the meal when everyone has a glass of champagne or has had their glasses refilled.

Toasts can also take place when all the guests are seated and have been served their drinks. At less formal affairs, toasts should be offered after everyone has gone through the receiving line and been served a drink.

Toasts are generally offered to the bride and groom by the best man, and the groom should respond with a toast of thanks. Other toasts may then be offered: the father of the bride, the mother of the bride, groom to bride, bride to groom. More often than not, however, the best man, the groom and father of the bride are the only three speakers.

Toasting guidelines

There are no hard and fast rules to toast-making and giving. What follows are guidelines to give you a starting point.

- **Be eloquent and witty.** Make sure that the toast you are delivering is appropriate to the intended audience and occasion.

- **Be simple**. Keep your toast short and to the point, and avoid using big words. The simplest words often sound the most sincere.

- **Be yourself**. Give it from the heart.

- **Be brief**. Avoid more than just a few sentences. Don't use the toast as a soapbox.

- **Be prepared**. A good toast is a speech in miniature. It takes far more work to craft a short message than a long speech. It takes practice to sound spontaneous.

- **End on a positive note**. Clearly define the end by saying, 'Cheers!', asking your audience to 'Raise your glass,' or some other accepted gesture.

Toasting etiquette and protocol

Here are some tips on accepted patterns of behavior when giving or receiving a toast.

- Never drink a toast, or stand up, when it's being offered to you. However, you should always stand up and respond to the toast, even if this means just thanking the host for the gesture.

- You should always stand when offering a toast unless it is a small informal group. Standing can help you to get the attention of the group and quieten them down.

- It is best not to signal for quiet by knocking on a glass with cutlery. You could easily end up with nothing to toast with.

- It is not a good idea to push someone to make a toast who would otherwise prefer not to. You might hear a toast that you would prefer not to.

- Never refuse to participate in a toast. It is more polite and per-fectly acceptable to participate with a non-alcoholic beverage or even an empty glass than not at all.

Alcohol concerns

Weddings have a tendency to create an atmosphere where over-drinking is tolerated. Of course it is natural to want to have a fabulous time, and drinking alcohol is a pleasurable way to share good times with friends and family. But binge-drinking is seen as almost acceptable in some societies especially, regrettably, in Britain, and I expect you don't want it to spoil your wedding.

Risks to your guests can include being insulted to being assaulted so keep a careful eye on drink and who may be in line to spoil the party.

Hints on how to avoid your guests over-indulging

If your guests over-indulge their behaviour might become intolerable, and they might suffer from alcohol poisoning. How can you avoid this?

- Make sure you offer plenty of food and water or soft drinks. These are some ways to help those hell-bent on taking advan-tage of free drinks.

- Limit the amount of alcohol you buy. Check the guidelines for the amount of wine and other drinks usually served at wedding under your drinks budget.

- Only have wines, beers and champagne or sparkling wines i.e. no spirits.

- Check the amount of alcohol content in the wines and beers you propose buying; if the wine is over 14% you might like to con-sider choosing ones with less.

- Offer bucks fizz or other diluted alcoholic drinks.

- Appoint a designated watcher. This could be an usher who keeps an eye out for any guests who are on the verge of get-ting drunk, and deals with the situation.

- Be responsible hosts. Make sure that no one gets in a car if they have been drinking.

Tip

The body can only process one unit of alcohol per hour. A unit is half a pint of beer or cider; a small glass of wine; a single measure of spirits. One unit is 10ml of pure alcohol. An alcopop, such as Smirnoff Ice, Bacardi Breezer, WKD or Reef is around 1.5 units.

9 Finding and managing your staff

This chapter covers your staffing requirements, be they professional or amateur, from an agency or from your address book. You need to know how many to have whoever you choose to help with the catering and drinks.

You may also be recruiting people to help with the car parking or other arrangements. The key to a good outcome is communication. You need to brief everyone on what you expect whether they are from an agency or have volunteered to help.

In this chapter I'll cover:

- finding staff

- calculating how many you need (both for the food and the bar)

- staff dress code and conduct

- how to instruct them

- taking care of the staff: their meals, breaks, tipping and being paid.

Finding staff and volunteers

Choosing the right people to help you in the run-up or on the day is crucial. Service, even by paid professionals and the public, is often seen as a menial job which can attract less than committed people, so vet your staff agency very thoroughly before signing a contract.

You are looking for helpful, professional, welcoming, knowledgeable staff who will give their all. You want to avoid shirkers, people on permanent fag breaks or those with attitude.

Where should you start looking for waiters, waitresses, bar staff and kitchen help? Here are some possible avenues to take:

- Friends and family.

- Agency staff.

- Talk to local catering colleges. Tutors are keen for their students to take on professional jobs while in training. You might recruit waiting and kitchen staff this way — and for the minimum wage or a package deal.

Agency staff

I have had a mixed bag of agency staff, from the downright surly to the couldn't-do-enough-for-guests professionalism that one expects from an agency which specialises in catering staff. As you will be paying a premium — agencies cream a lot off what they pay their staff — you can rightly expect top quality. Talk to people who have hired staff via this method, talk to the agency regarding their staff's qualifications and experience and find out about all charges before signing on the dotted line.

Agencies will charge higher rates on weekends and holidays. They will also charge you for travel and for meals (depending on the length of time you wish to employ their staff). Make absolutely sure when hiring agency staff that they speak the language you need, who the team leader is, the numbers of breaks they can have and the exact duties they are expected to carry out. Also determine their uniform. If you are not happy about excess jewellery or make-up, discuss this with the agency beforehand and make sure that these points are written up in the contract before you sign it.

Types of staff and duties

You could hire the following from an agency:

- bartender
- bar staff
- waiting staff

- kitchen staff – who will be in charge of the washing up or as kitchen assistants.

You may wish them to do the following:

- welcoming your guests
- setting tables, laying crockery, cutlery and glasses
- serving food and drinks
- laying out buffets or serving tables
- setting bar and preparing cocktails
- keeping the place clean and tidy throughout the event
- clearing up and washing up at the end of the event.

Questions to ask an agency

- What is your charge per hour? Does this include VAT?
- Is there an extra charge for weekend or holiday work?
- Is there a transport charge?
- How much experience do your staff have?
- Are they trained or just casual labour?
- How many hours can they work?
- Do you charge for overtime?
- What can they expect for breaks?
- What will they expect to eat?
- Can I have non-smoking staff only?
- How much importance does the company attach to grooming?

- What do staff wear? (You can stipulate your demands here.)

- Do they speak English? (Or whatever language you prefer.)

- Can I have all the details in writing?

- When do you expect payment?

- If I am dissatisfied with your staff for any reason how can this be addressed?

Staff costs

Below are some ballpark 2008 figures for staff costs. These are exclusive of VAT and travel.

- Qualified chefs: £27 per hour

- Waitresses and waiters £11.50 per hour

- Bar staff £12.50 per hour

- Kitchen porters £10.50 per hour.

In addition, note that a minimum of six hours may be charged for any chefs. Also, between 11pm and 6am, time and a half may apply. Bank holidays may be charged at double time.

Tip

Pay your staff on the night, if hiring casual staff, either by cheque or cash. Check the hours they are claiming. When dealing with agency staff, the staff member who is in charge will give you a time sheet to sign. Make sure it is accurate as you may not be able to change any details after the event. Payment to an agency often takes place in two parts: a deposit and a final invoice.

Tip

You may wish to add a tip to those who have served you well. Give them cash in hand rather than adding it on to the bill if you have chosen staff via an agency. Catering students or other staff chosen by you will also be delighted by a tip. Ensure that you have sufficient cash for all concerned when giving it out — plan ahead a little.

National minimum wage

The minimum wage is a legal right. The rates, effective from 1 October 2007 are:

- £5.52 an hour for workers over 22 years old
- £4.60 for workers aged 18–21
- £3.40 an hour for workers aged 16–17 years old.

It is a criminal offence to refuse to pay the minimum wage, with fines up to £5,000.

Tip

If employing kitchen and waiting staff make sure they all know what each other is doing and respect each other's jobs. Establish a harmonious atmosphere and tackle any unpleasant attitudes if and when they become apparent.

Friends and family as helpers

If you are asking friends and family to help before and on the day make sure that they know their roles. Will you be paying them or are they giving their services free as a kind of wedding gift to you? Make sure you establish this beforehand or bad feelings might be the result. You may wish to offer the younger members some form of payment such as a specific sum rather than a per hour rate. But make sure that you establish the following first:

- What duties will you ask them to carry out?

- What responsibilities will you give them?

- What will you ask them to wear?

- What will you do about meals, drinking and smoking?

Family and friends are often more than willing to lend a hand in whatever way they can to make sure that the day passes off smoothly. However, they do need guidance and roles. Establish these beforehand or you may find that too many people are doing the same jobs while others are ignored. As a final tip, I have found in the past that friends and family do volunteer but are often caught up in conversation, forgetting to help. This is particularly the case later on in the event, when the washing up and tidying away gets left for a few to do. (If friends and family do help, they must be made aware of food storage, hygiene and smoking.)

Catering colleges

Many students studying catering take on work above and beyond college work to gain experience. But, as with any other group of people, some have natural abilities, while others have strengths elsewhere. Talk to the head of department regarding your needs and he or she will guide you to the right students. You will need to have a good idea of the hours required, their duties, their payment, travel costs if applicable, where they can park and what you expect them to wear.

Staff hygiene

All staff, whether they are from colleges or staff agencies or people who you have taken on from other sources should have short, clean, unvarnished nails. They must also wash their hands after a cigarette break, or going to the toilet or after handling boxes or other equipment.

They should also have clean chefs' jackets, aprons, head gear and any other items of uniform, and not wear excess jewellery.

Tip

Be firm regarding smoking breaks. Talk to whoever you employ beforehand, laying down these and other requirements of service. Staff can smoke in their own time when not working, otherwise it is unfair on non-smokers who will have to work more as a result. It is also unpleasant for your guests to smell smoke on a member of staff's hands, clothes or breath. It can ruin food and wine. Unfortunately there are too many smokers in the catering trade.

Staff numbers

Some staffing logistics are quite daunting. The Queen's garden parties are huge affairs: a typical garden party serves around 27,000 cups of tea, 20,000 sandwiches and 20,000 slices of cake. Some 400 waiting staff are involved in the serving.

Your needs are more modest — thankfully, I hear you say! Here are some guidelines to help you on your way. They are just a guide which you may need to adapt if you are arranging a different type of wedding party with the emphasis on drink rather than food. Or you may want a less formal approach, with guests helping themselves and participating in the serving, pouring and washing up. Alter the guide to suit you. Do bear in mind that you may also not have the professionalism if you employ amateurs.

- Formal seated dinners: one waiting staff per ten guests.
- Seated buffets: one waiting staff per 20 guests. This does not include servers or any kitchen staff.
- Canapé and drinks wedding receptions: one bar person and three waiting staff per 50 guests.

Professional waiting skills

If you are not in the business you may not be aware of the following. It's a good idea to pass these tips on to those helping you:

- Serve from the left and remove from the right.
- Hold the plate by placing four fingers under it with the thumb on the side, not on the surface, of the plate.
- When holding two plates in one hand, balance one plate on the forearm by the wrist, with three fingers under the top plate, and the thumb and small finger on the rim of the lower plates.
- Clear plates by balancing one plate (as above) for cutlery. That way the stronger part of the forearm and wrist bear the weight of the cleared plates.
- Serve drinks on the right where the glass is positioned.
- Always hold the glasses by the stem, never the bowl.
- Clear the table after each course, leaving it set for the next course. This means removing salt and pepper shakers, side plates, butter dishes and surplus cutlery, for example, before serving the dessert.

- Clear plates when everyone at the table has finished eating. If you don't wait you're implying that the guests should get a move on! If you clear at different times this makes slower eaters at the table feel awkward.

Briefing waiting and kitchen staff

These guidelines will help you decide when to get your staff together and how to manage them. You need to tell them:

- they should arrive two hours before a large wedding, such as a buffet or sit down dinner, less for a finger food reception

- they should also stay for at least half an hour after the last guest has left to clear everything up

- the timings of guests' arrival, meal service and the expected end time of the event

- the number of guests

- the menu and any special catering requirements such as vegetarian, vegan, gluten-free or dairy-free meals and which guests they are for

- the drinks and wines to serve, or to keep replenishing tables with bottles for guests to help themselves

- any special items such as name place cards or seating plan

- where all the equipment is to be found and what to do with dirty plates on clearing away

- where coffee or tea is to be served (at the tables or on the buffet?)

- where coats and hats are stored as well as wedding gifts guests might bring

- where they can leave their belongings

- where the toilets are

- what the staff will have to eat and when they can take a break.

Remind them to:

- set up the bar and tables

- clear ashtrays and replace them (this now applies to outside in most cases)

- clear pre-meal glasses

- clear any area used at the end of the party.

Tip

You may find it useful to have a printed sheet of duties, plus the menu and timings, pinned up in the kitchen area so that staff can refresh their memories if they didn't take everything in at the briefing.

---

10 After the party

The wedding has been a success. You've all enjoyed the fruits of your labours and those of others who have played their part in making your day a memorable one — for all the right reasons!

But there are always loose ends to tidy up. When will the marquee be dismantled? How will I get the equipment back to the hire company or will they pick it up? Which bills are still outstanding? What are the terms of agreement?

You may also have to knuckle down to writing all those thank you notes or letters after the honeymoon if you have decided to have one. Have you kept some cake to send to those unable to attend due to other commitments or poor health?

This chapter covers these points and others including arranging a post-wedding party or a drinks party for those not invited to the wedding.

You may also be interested in the reasons for certain wedding customs in Britain and in other countries. These and myths are outlined here too, with possible ideas to incorporate into your wedding plans.

Sorting out the marquee and equipment

Let's look at what needs to be done, either by you or by others when you're on your honeymoon.

The marquee

When organising the marquee, arrange the dismantling of the marquee, the date and time. Make sure that the company complies with your requests for the garden or area to be left as they found it with no upturned turf, pegs left in the ground, damaged trees, bushes or flowerbeds. If a problem is found, contact the company immediately so that they can come to sort it out.

The equipment

If you have hired equipment such as tables, chairs, plates, cutlery, glasses and other items, ensure that those who have been left to deal with it in your absence know who to contact if the equipment hasn't been collected on the arranged date. Ensure too that the equipment list has been ticked off with all items accounted for. A separate list of missing items should be made and the company informed of losses. Otherwise you won't have much of a case if the company charges you for items you think have been collected or returned. As with the marquee hire company, make sure that those dealing with the equipment return in your absence know the contact details.

Suppliers: outstanding bills to pay

Before the wedding takes place, go through the list of suppliers and write down the payments made, how much is due and when all payments are to be paid. The following may be included:

- caterers
- drinks suppliers (you may have wine or other drinks on a sale or return basis if whole cases, for example, haven't been opened)
- venue
- cake maker
- toastmaster
- musicians or other entertainment
- florists
- photographer
- marquee company

- equipment hire company
- staff agency
- car hire company
- clothing hire company (you may have hired morning coats and hats, for example).

Making a complaint to suppliers

You will have paid the printers and possibly others already on the above list — or you may have paid a deposit, the balance still outstanding. If you have any issues with any services contact them immediately, and preferably in writing, stating your dissatisfaction or grievance. If you don't address the problem within a reasonable time span, you may be required to pay the entire amount you agreed. Put your case clearly and succinctly.

Alternatively, before you sign a contract with a company, you may wish to contact your local authority to ascertain the company's credibility, (see below). If you do have a problem after the event, contact Consumer Direct (see below). Below is advice given by the website oft.gov.uk

Assured trader schemes

Many local authorities run assured trader schemes. They aim to give consumers a reliable way of finding trustworthy local businesses.

Businesses that sign up to the schemes get support and promotion from their local authority trading standards services, in return for a promise that they will meet their legal obligations and treat their customers fairly.

Most schemes have been developed separately, and vary in the details of how they work. But all the Local Authority Assured Trader Scheme Network (LAATSN) member schemes have the common aims of:

- giving consumers a reliable way of finding businesses they can trust

- offering a source of help and advice if things go wrong

- enabling local businesses to demonstrate that they have signed up to national standards.

The Local Authority Assured Trader Scheme Network

As the national champion of local authority trading standards services, the Office of Fair Trading (OFT) supports a network of local authority local trader schemes which meet nationally agreed standards. The Local Authority Assured Trader Scheme Network aims to bring greater consistency to local schemes, and to promote the value of local schemes to those who stand to benefit most — local consumers and businesses.

Empowering consumers to make informed choices when buying goods and services is a common aim across national and local governments. So there are several schemes designed to help consumers. The schemes all aim to drive up business standards and boost customer confidence. It comes under the banner of the Consumer Codes Approval Scheme. If a business displays the OFT Approved code logo you can have confidence that they:

- are committed to treat you fairly if problems arise

- will guarantee good customer service

- give clear-cut information about the goods or services they're selling

- give user-friendly, straightforward and quick procedures for dealing with customer complaints

- will offer free or low cost dispute resolution, such as arbitration or an ombudsman, if you can't agree about how to sort out a problem

- will offer you more rights than the law gives you.

If you feel you have been treated unfairly contact your local authority or the ombudsman who will be able to assess the situation and arbritrate on your behalf if you are seen as having a case.

Consumer Direct

Consumer Direct is a government funded organisation which offers clear, practical consumer advice. Its services include:

- providing pre-shopping advice before you buy goods or services

- explaining your consumer rights

- advising you if you have a problem or disagreement with a trader

- helping you make a complaint about a trader that you believe has done something wrong (although will not complain on your behalf)

- providing general advice on how to avoid unscrupulous traders or 'cowboys'

- explaining consumer-related issues such as warranties, buying on credit, internet shopping, refunds and replacements, etc

- providing advice on avoiding trading scams and rip-offs

- directing you to a regulator or other organisation if it is better suited to assist you

- refering your case to your local authority Trading Standards Services or similar agency if they are better suited to assist you.

Consumer Direct will deal with each caller's problems or questions individually. They will provide an honest, impartial assessment of the situation and where possible, will recommend a clear course of action to follow. They can only provide information and advice. They cannot intervene directly in consumer matters, such as taking action against a trader.

If it is appropriate, they may forward the details of a complaint to an agency that is authorised to take direct action, such as Trading Standards Services. You do not have to provide personal details to use the Consumer Direct service. However, this may affect the way they handle your query or complaint.

What Consumer Direct don't do (amongst other things which are not pertinent to this book):

- Recommend a trader or organisation (but they may direct you to another organisation that has helpful information).

- Give specific information about whether there has been a complaint about a trader.

- Complain to a trader on your behalf.

- Provide advice on specific products (except in relation to safety issues).

- Consumer Direct is not a legal service. However, their advisers are trained in all aspects of consumer rights. This enables them to offer legally correct advice and courses of action that consumers can rely on.

www.consumerdirect.gov.uk 08454 04 05 06.

Tip

It may not be worth making a fuss if a small amount of money is the cause of your grievance. Pay up and put it behind you. But do contact your local trading standards office if you have a major grievance.

Thank you letters

Compile a list of those who you wish to thank for their part in making the wedding a success; those who have given presents or their time. A small handwritten card is perfectly acceptable but do specify what you are thanking them for. It can be hard for some people to accept the fact that you haven't a clue what they chose, wrapped with care and gave to you. Be specific in your thanks, but be succinct as you may have many cards to write. Of course some cards may become detached from gifts. This can be a problem. But be up front about it — ask around and you may find out who the donor is. These things happen.

Tip

Writing thank you notes is a joint effort on the part of the bride and groom, not just for the bride. Start as you mean to go on!

Cake boxes

A very nice gesture is to send a piece of cake in a small, celebratory box to those unable to attend the wedding — or those who weren't invited but are on your guest list for a post-wedding drinks party. These boxes can be obtained at cake shops, card shops and businesses via the internet or printers. They often have space for the name, address and stamp with a small card placed inside the box to denote who sent it or they can be put in an envelope with a covering note.

Make sure that the type of cake will withstand the journey and the elements; a fruit cake is the ideal type to send. Delegate a family member or friend to cut up the cake and post the boxes for you if you are on your honeymoon. Make sure you leave a legible list of names, addresses and appropriate stamps for this to be carried out without a hitch.

Post-wedding celebratory party

As mentioned in Chapter 6, you may have decided on a smaller wedding if the numbers, and therefore costs per head, are high. You can invite others not on the list to a post-wedding party. This could take place within a few weeks of the actual ceremony and be a drinks party with finger food or a simple barbecue with music. Or you may decide on a dance, a picnic on a beach or hilltop or in a pub with a party room with live music.

You may decide to have a post-wedding party for several other reasons too. Perhaps you had a small, family gathering and would like to invite a larger crowd to celebrate with you. You may have had an intimate dinner after your wedding abroad, with a larger party to follow. You might have eloped with no one attending your wedding. There are many other possible reasons for not having a wedding to which friends and family were invited. Very occasionally a bereavement in the family makes it impossible to celebrate.

Other party possibilities which are outlined in Chapter 6 include:

- drinks with music
- buffet — out or indoors
- finger food reception
- champagne tea party.

Appendix

Wedding traditions and symbols

Weddings throughout history have left their mark on how we and other cultures organise our weddings. Here are some British and other European traditions still very much in place in today's society, the traditionalist in us all coming out when planning a wedding:

- Wearing something old: if the bride wears a piece of family jewellery or her mother's or grandmother's wedding dress it represents links with the bride's family and the past.

- Wearing something new: this represents good fortune and success in the bride's new life.

- Something borrowed: to remind the bride that friends and family will be there for her when help is needed. It could be represented by a lace handkerchief or a piece of jewellery.

- Something blue: this symbolises faithfulness and loyalty. It dates back to biblical times when blue represented fidelity, the garter often blue.

- Silver sixpence: worn in the bride's shoe to wish her financial wealth and happiness.

- Wedding veil: the veil hides the bride's beauty and wards off evil spirits.

- Anne of Brittany started the tradition of wearing a white wedding dress in the 15th century, white denoting joy, not purity as is commonly thought.

- Position of the bride and groom at the altar: the bride stands on the left of the groom during the marriage ceremony to allow his sword arm to be free ready to fight off other men who may want her as their bride.

- Confetti has replaced rice or grain, thrown at the couple to encourage fertility.

- Wedding gifts: gifts have replaced the custom of guests bringing fruit to encourage fertility.

- Dropping the wedding ring shakes out the evil spirits.

- The couple should exchange wedding vows as the clock's hand is ascending towards heaven.

- The arch of swords through which the couple walk after the ceremony denotes their safe passage into their new life together.

- The wedding cake is cut by the bride and groom to represent sharing their life together.

- Shoes were a powerful symbol in ancient times, the tying of shoes to cars carrying on this tradition.

- Carrying the bride over the threshold protects her from evil spirits.

With thanks to the website www.hitched.co.uk for the above information and to Julie Cox for the traditions outlined below both of which have been abridged.

British and other wedding traditions from around the world

In the Middle Ages the woman was often 'kidnapped' by her groom, the man, accompanied by his best friend standing by in case of a fight breaking out. This led to the tradition of the Best Man to stand by the groom to protect him and look after him.

Gold rings were used as currency, the man paying for his bride in gold, the currency going to the family. Gimmal rings or three interlocking rings, were separated in Elizabethan times, one worn by the bride, the groom and their witness during the engagement. On the wedding day all three rings were united as a single ring for the bride.

Choosing the day on which to marry was considered very important. Based on a pagan rhyme, Monday was for health, Tuesday for wealth, Wednesday best of all, Thursday for losses, Friday for crosses, Saturday for no luck at all.

Seating in the church is also symbolic, the bride's family on one side, the groom on the other. This goes back to times when a girl of one tribe was offered by her father as a peace offering to another tribe, keeping them apart a safety precaution.

French traditions

The traditional bridal trousseau originated in France, the word 'trousse' coming from 'bundle'.

Still practiced in small villages today, the groom calls on his future wife at her home on the day of the wedding to escort her to church. At the church, the village children stretch white ribbons across the road which the bride cuts. When the couple leave the church or the mairie or town hall, laurel leaves are scattered in their path.

After the wedding reception or later in the evening, friends of the couple might show up outside their window banging pots and pans, singing bois-terous songs. The groom is expected to invite them in for drinks and snacks.

Spanish traditions

Orange blossoms have long been the flower of choice for a bride as the orange tree bears fruit and blossoms at the same time its flowers repre-sent happiness and fulfilment.

Before a couple gets married, they exchange their vows in church, the groom giving his bride a wedding present of thirteen coins. This gift is a symbol of his commitment to support her. The bride-to-be then carries these coins, in a little bag, to her wedding ceremony.

According to Spanish custom, a Spanish bride wore, and still might wear, a black silk wedding dress with an intricately designed black lace veil. Her groom usually wears an embroidered shirt, hand made by his future wife.

During a Spanish marriage celebration reception guests traditionally dance a 'sequidillas manchegas' and present the newlyweds with a gift.

Italian traditions

Italian weddings, in times past, were arranged by the families of the bride and groom, in some cases a matchmaker sending a message to the prospective bride's family of the man's intent to marry the bride.

If the groom proposed directly to the bride, he would serenade her first, either playing an instrument or turning up with musician friends.

Wearing green by the bridge the night before the wedding brings luck and abundance to the couple.

On the day of the wedding the bride is not to wear gold until she is given her gold wedding ring.

Old church traditions forbade marriage in the months of May and August, May reserved for the veneration of the Virgin Mary, August thought to invite bad luck and sickness. Sunday marriages are believed to be luckiest.

In southern regions of Italy the couple breaks a vase or glass into many pieces at the end of the wedding day, the number of pieces representing the number of years of happy married life.

Italian weddings always emphasise food. Strongly linked with family life, food is the focal point of the festivities.

Russian traditions

Russian wedding protocol is quite different from other marriage ceremonies in the world with no bridesmaids, best man or flower girl amongst other examples.

There is no engagement in Russia. Once the couple decide to marry they will do so within one to three months. The department of registrations will offer them dates, the couple are then considered as being bride and groom.

The wedding ring is worn on the right hand, a ring worn on the left hand signalling a widowed or divorced person.

A Russian wedding usually lasts for two days but can stretch up to a week. No Russian wedding party is complete without a series of toasts or gor'kos. The second day of the wedding is held at the home of the couple with many games including guests messing the floor for the bride to clean up, the 'mess' money, coins or banknotes.

Traditionally the wedding is ruled by witnesses who must prepare a script for the wedding so that the guests are entertained all the time, fun being the main reason for the wedding.

Nowadays many couples opt for a church marriage but they still do not have official status and the couple must be married at the registration office before the marriage in church. The Russian church ceremony is colourful and solemn — and very long. Guests and the couple stand during the ceremony as there is no seating in Russian churches.

Chinese traditions

Many traditional rituals and customs have been lost in the course of history but some are still observed. They are practised in honour of family values and respect to committed relationships, a marriage considered the joining of two families.

Both families are involved in the wedding planning from the start, both picking an auspicious date as the Betrothal Day. The groom's family presents various proposal gifts that represent fertility and prosperity, all gifts coming in even numbers meaning 'good things double' in Chinese culture.

Wedding cakes are sent out with the invitations to the wedding, with dragon and phoenix emblems on the cakes.

The two families decorate the bridal house and the reception venue with lots of lively colours, red in particular. Banners are written with rhythmic poems praising the couple and the perfect marriage.

On the morning of the wedding day, the hair dressing ritual is performed for the bride, her hair is done up in a bun with auspicious words being spoken. There are many games including the Door Games — the groom arrives at the bride's house and the bridemaids will ask him questions about the bride to try to delay her being married. The bride is covered by a red umbrella when she finally leaves the house to protect her from evil spirits.

The Chinese wedding tea ceremony: the couple kneel three times — to heaven and earth, to the ancestral tablets and their parents, then to each other. Bowing has replaced this in many areas. The bride then presents tea to the parents and relatives in order of seniority, the recipients usually giving gifts wrapped in red envelopes.

The wedding food is highly symbolic, a roast suckling pig denoting the bride's virginity, pigeon denoting a peaceful future. Chicken cooked in red oil symbolises the wish for a prosperous life, lobster, equally playing a part. Both these dishes indicate that the dragon (lobster) and phoenix (chicken) are in harmony, the yin and yang elements balanced for this family.

In a modern Chinese wedding the bride changes dresses three times: a western-style white wedding dress for the ceremony, a traditional Chinese bridal dress for the tea ceremony and the reception and a cocktail dress at the end of the banquet. This dress is known as the 'Song Ke' or seeing guests off dress.

Index

Index